LATIN AMERICAN POLITICAL, ECONOMIC, AND SECURITY ISSUES



# UNACCOMPANIED CHILDREN FROM CENTRAL AMERICA

## ISSUES AND CONSIDERATIONS

# LATIN AMERICAN POLITICAL, ECONOMIC, AND SECURITY ISSUES

Additional books in this series can be found on Nova's website under the Series tab.

Additional e-books in this series can be found on Nova's website under the e-book tab.

LATIN AMERICAN POLITICAL, ECONOMIC, AND SECURITY ISSUES

# UNACCOMPANIED CHILDREN FROM CENTRAL AMERICA

## ISSUES AND CONSIDERATIONS

VERONICA K. QUINN
EDITOR

NOVINKA

*New York*

**Library of Congress Cataloging-in-Publication Data**

ISBN: 978-1-63482-937-3

*Published by Nova Science Publishers, Inc. † New York*

# Contents


| | | |
|---|---|---|
| **Preface** | | **vii** |
| **Chapter 1** | Central America: Information on Migration of Unaccompanied Children from El Salvador, Guatemala, and Honduras<br>*United States Government Accountability Office* | **1** |
| **Chapter 2** | Unaccompanied Alien Children: Demographics in Brief<br>*Ruth Ellen Wasem and Austin Morris* | **23** |
| **Chapter 3** | Unaccompanied Children from Central America: Foreign Policy Considerations<br>*Peter J. Meyer, Clare Ribando Seelke, Maureen Taft-Morales and Rhoda Margesson* | **35** |
| **Chapter 4** | Testimony of Elizabeth Hogan, Senior Deputy Assistant for Latin America and the Caribbean, USAID. Hearing on "Unaccompanied Alien Children: Pressing the Administration for a Strategy" | **69** |
| **Chapter 5** | Testimony of Roberta S. Jacobson, Assistant Secretary of State, Bureau of Western Hemisphere Affairs, U.S. Department of State. Hearing on "Unaccompanied Alien Children: Pressing the Administration for a Strategy" | **75** |

**Chapter 6** Testimony of Robert N. Kaplan, President and CEO, Inter-American Foundation. Hearing on "Unaccompanied Alien Children: Pressing the Administration for a Strategy" **81**

**Index** **89**

# PREFACE

Since 2012, there has been a rapid increase in the number of unaccompanied alien children (UAC) apprehended at the U.S.-Mexican border. According to DHS's Customs and Border Protection (CBP), the number of UAC from any country apprehended at the U.S.-Mexican border climbed from more than 24,000 in fiscal year 2012 to nearly 39,000 in fiscal year 2013, and to nearly 69,000 in fiscal year 2014. Prior to fiscal year 2012, the majority of UAC apprehended at the border were Mexican nationals. However, more than half of the UAC apprehended at the border in fiscal year 2013, and 75 percent apprehended in fiscal year 2014 were nationals of El Salvador, Guatemala, and Honduras, according to DHS/CBP. El Salvador, Guatemala, and Honduras face various socioeconomic challenges, which the United States is seeking to address through assistance efforts. This book identifies U.S. mission-level efforts to identify causes of the rapid increase in migration of unaccompanied children and address the causes identified. Furthermore, this book discusses the demographics of unaccompanied alien children while they are in removal proceedings.

In: Unaccompanied Children from Central America ISBN: 978-1-63482-937-3
Editor: Veronica K. Quinn 

*Chapter 1*

# CENTRAL AMERICA: INFORMATION ON MIGRATION OF UNACCOMPANIED CHILDREN FROM EL SALVADOR, GUATEMALA, AND HONDURAS*

***United States Government Accountability Office***

## ABBREVIATIONS

| | |
|---|---|
| CARSI | Central America Regional Security Initiative |
| CBP | Customs and Border Protection |
| DHS | Department of Homeland Security |
| UAC | unaccompanied alien children |
| USAID | U.S. Agency for International Development |

## WHY GAO DID THIS STUDY

Since 2012, there has been a rapid increase in the number of UAC apprehended at the U.S.-Mexican border. According to DHS's Customs and Border Protection (CBP), the number of UAC from any country apprehended

* This is an edited, reformatted and augmented version of The United States Government Accountability Office publication, GAO-15-362, dated February 2015.

at the U.S.-Mexican border climbed from more than 24,000 in fiscal year 2012 to nearly 39,000 in fiscal year 2013, and to nearly 69,000 in fiscal year 2014. Prior to fiscal year 2012, the majority of UAC apprehended at the border were Mexican nationals. However, more than half of the UAC apprehended at the border in fiscal year 2013, and 75 percent apprehended in fiscal year 2014 were nationals of El Salvador, Guatemala, and Honduras, according to DHS/CBP. El Salvador, Guatemala, and Honduras face various socioeconomic challenges, which the United States is seeking to address through assistance efforts.

GAO was asked to review issues related to U.S. assistance to Central America addressing the rapid increase in migration of UAC from El Salvador, Guatemala, and Honduras to the United States. This report identifies U.S. mission-level efforts to (1) identify causes of the rapid increase in migration of unaccompanied children and (2) address the causes identified.

GAO developed a set of questions to obtain written responses from State, USAID, and DHS officials responsible for programs in El Salvador, Guatemala, and Honduras. GAO reviewed, analyzed, and tabulated these agency officials' responses.

## What GAO Found

Department of State (State), U.S. Agency for International Development (USAID), and Department of Homeland Security (DHS) officials stationed in El Salvador, Guatemala, and Honduras most commonly identified crime and violence and economic concerns as causes primarily responsible for the recent rapid increase in migration to the United States by unaccompanied alien children (UAC). These causes were followed by educational concerns, the desire for family reunification, and the role of smuggling networks, among others. Agency officials' responses to a GAO set of questions showed little variance in attributing causes of UAC migration by country. The officials reported drawing on various sources of information to identify these causes, including conducting first-hand interviews with migrants and their families; meeting with host government and non-governmental agencies; and analyzing various data, reports, and other information sources. For example, the State and USAID officials' responses for Honduras noted that the agencies had identified causes through a combination of surveys, discussions with government agencies and civil society organizations, anecdotal reports, and others.

The officials reported that agencies had developed new programs and modified existing programs to address the rapid increase in UAC migration in each of the three countries. They noted that most of these programs are specifically targeted to address identified causes of migration, such as crime and violence, lack of economic opportunities, and criminal networks that smuggle unaccompanied children. For example, DHS officials reported that the department had implemented Operation Coyote, an initiative active in all three countries to combat criminal organizations involved in UAC smuggling. According to agency officials, new and modified programs ranged in location from specific communities or cities to border areas to nation-wide or region-wide initiatives. State and USAID officials also noted that some of their efforts and strategic objectives that had been in place prior to the rapid increase in UAC migration focused on related issues such as economic development and crime reduction. Officials reported that they have undertaken various efforts to plan their responses to the increase in migration, including coordinating among U.S. agencies and with host governments. For example, agency officials from all three countries reported participating in UAC interagency working groups at each embassy. In addition, State and USAID officials said they have used DHS data on the location of origins of UAC to inform their efforts.

* * *

February 27, 2015

Congressional Requesters:

Since 2012, there has been a rapid increase in the number of unaccompanied alien children (UAC) apprehended at the U.S.-Mexican border.[1] According to the Department of Homeland Security's (DHS) Customs and Border Protection (CBP), the number of UAC from any country apprehended at the U.S.-Mexican border climbed from more than 24,000 in fiscal year 2012 to nearly 39,000 in fiscal year 2013, and to nearly 69,000 in fiscal year 2014. Prior to fiscal year 2012, the majority of UAC apprehended at the border were Mexican nationals. However, more than half of the UAC apprehended at the border in fiscal year 2013, and about 75 percent (nearly 51,000) of UAC apprehended in fiscal year 2014, were nationals of El Salvador, Guatemala, and Honduras, according to DHS/CBP.

El Salvador, Guatemala, and Honduras face various socioeconomic challenges, which the United States is seeking to address through assistance efforts. In fiscal year 2014, U.S. Agency for International Development (USAID) and State Department (State) bilateral assistance was about $22 million to El Salvador, $60 million to Guatemala, and $42 million to Honduras. The U.S. government also provides additional assistance through regional programs, such as the Central America Regional Security Initiative (CARSI). In addition, the Millennium Challenge Corporation has a $277 million compact with El Salvador and a $15.7 million threshold program with Honduras.[2]

We were asked to review issues related to U.S. assistance to Central America addressing the rapid increase in migration of UAC from El Salvador, Guatemala, and Honduras to the United States. This report identifies U.S. mission-level efforts to (1) identify causes of the rapid increase in migration of unaccompanied children and (2) address the causes identified. We will be issuing a separate report at a later date that examines agencies' assistance targeting and performance evaluation.

To address the objectives for this review, we developed a set of questions to obtain written responses from State, USAID, and DHS officials responsible for programs in El Salvador, Guatemala, and Honduras.[3] Specifically, we obtained responses reflecting the perspectives of the three ambassadors, regarding State efforts; the three mission directors, regarding USAID efforts; and the three country attachés, regarding DHS efforts. We reviewed, analyzed, and tabulated all agency responses.

We conducted this performance audit from September 2014 to February 2015 in accordance with generally accepted government auditing standards. Those standards require that we plan and perform the audit to obtain sufficient, appropriate evidence to provide a reasonable basis for our findings and conclusions based on our audit objectives. We believe that the evidence obtained provides a reasonable basis for our findings and conclusions based on our audit objectives.

## BACKGROUND

El Salvador, Guatemala, and Honduras—the countries with the greatest increase in migrating UAC—face numerous socioeconomic challenges. According to the United Nations Office on Drugs and Crime, these countries were among the top five countries with the highest homicide rates worldwide in 2012. In addition, according to 2011 World Bank data, more than 60 percent of Hondurans, more than 50 percent of Guatemalans, and 30 percent of Salvadorans live below the poverty level. Moreover, government officials from the three countries noted in their 2014 regional plan that income inequality presents a major challenge, as 20 percent of the wealthiest segments of the population account for more than half of overall income.[4] These officials also identified a limited supply and quality of services in housing, early childhood health care, nutrition, and child development as among the main challenges to development, while also noting that weaknesses in the countries' educational systems have resulted in workforces with less schooling and more limited skills as compared with those of other countries in the region. Finally, all three countries rank below the regional average on Transparency International's Corruption Perception Index.[5]

In fiscal years 2013 and 2014, combined, State and USAID bilateral assistance was about $49 million for El Salvador, more than $141 million for Guatemala, and more than $93 million for Honduras. The U.S. government also provides additional assistance through regional programs, such as CARSI. CARSI funds activities to improve law enforcement capabilities, prevent crime and violence, and deter and detect border criminal activity, among other efforts, in Belize, Costa Rica, El Salvador, Guatemala, Honduras, Nicaragua, and Panama. Between fiscal years 2008 and 2014, U.S. agencies allocated more than $800 million for CARSI activities from various accounts. We previously reported that, through June 2013, more than 50 percent of funds allocated for CARSI activities had been designated for activities in El Salvador, Guatemala, and Honduras.[6] In addition, the Millennium Challenge Corporation signed a $277 million compact with El Salvador in September 2014, with projects aimed at investing in El Salvador's regulatory systems to enhance investment opportunities, in human capital to improve the quality of education, and in physical capital to reduce transportation and logistics costs. The corporation also has a $15.7 million threshold program with Honduras, with projects to increase the efficiency and transparency of public financial management and public-private partnerships.

The administration has taken recent action related to these three countries. On November 14, 2014, the administration announced an in-country refugee/parole program in El Salvador, Guatemala, and Honduras, which has since begun. The program is intended to allow certain parents who are lawfully present in the United States to request access to the U.S. Refugee

Admissions Program for their children still living in El Salvador, Guatemala, and Honduras.

## AGENCY OFFICIALS MOST COMMONLY IDENTIFIED VIOLENCE AND ECONOMIC CONCERNS AMONG THE CAUSES OF UNACCOMPANIED CHILD MIGRATION TO THE UNITED STATES

State, USAID, and DHS officials stationed in El Salvador, Guatemala, and Honduras most commonly identified crime and violence and economic concerns as causes primarily responsible for the rapid increase in UAC migration to the United States, followed by educational concerns, the desire for family reunification, and the role of smuggling networks. Family dysfunction and migrants' perceptions of U.S. immigration policy were among other causes the agency officials identified. A State official noted that individual migrants are likely to be driven to migrate by a mixture of these causes. The responses showed little variance in attributing the causes of migration by country. Agency officials reported drawing on various sources of information to identify these causes, ranging from conducting first-hand interviews to analyzing various statistical data.

- Crime and violence: All nine of the State, USAID, and DHS officials' responses identified crime and violence as a cause. Agency officials' responses noted that gangs, drug trafficking, and criminal organizations contributed to the crime and violence. For example, the State official's response for Honduras noted that gang activities, such spread of the coffee rust fungus, which has increased in the past 2 years and has hurt coffee production.7 Specifically, the USAID official's response reported that the fungus has affected 70 percent of Guatemala's coffee crop and resulted in the loss of 100,000 jobs and a reduction in coffee output of 15 percent. The State official's response for Honduras also noted that high income disparity and unemployment affect urban areas as well.
- Educational concerns: Eight of nine State, USAID, and DHS officials' responses identified educational concerns, including low quality of or limited access to education, as a cause. Most agency officials' responses identified economic and educational concerns as

interconnected causes of migration. For example, USAID officials' responses noted that in El Salvador the poorly performing educational system fails to provide the necessary skills for children to obtain jobs, leading to increased migration, while in Honduras, youth who work or go to school generally are less likely to consider migrating.

- Family reunification: Eight of nine State, USAID, and DHS officials' responses identified the desire to reunify with family as a cause. The State official's response for Guatemala noted that unaccompanied child migrants may seek to reunify with a parent or family member in the United States, while the State official's response for Honduras noted the desire for reunification and the belief that minors would be allowed to remain in the United States indefinitely increased the migration of unaccompanied children.
- Role of smuggling organizations: Eight of nine State, USAID, and DHS officials' responses identified the role of smuggling networks as a cause. Agency officials responded that human smugglers have increasingly influenced the rate of migration through more aggressive and misleading marketing approaches. For example, the State official's response for El Salvador noted that smugglers increased migration demand this past summer by providing false or misleading information on the ease of migration. The State official's response for Guatemala noted these same tactics by smugglers, along with rising crime and an improving U.S economy, likely drove this summer's increase of UAC migrants from Guatemala. The State official's response for Honduras noted that smugglers increased their recruiting of child migrants in the spring of 2014, taking advantage of Hondurans' desire to reunite with family members in the United States, as well as Hondurans' perceptions that changes in U.S. immigration law would ease paths to citizenship for Hondurans in the United States. USAID and DHS officials' responses for El Salvador described increasing efforts by smugglers to employ savvy marketing tactics in appealing to youth and their families.
- Domestic dysfunction or abuse: Family dysfunction, breakdowns in family structures, or domestic abuse was identified as a cause in six agency officials' responses across all three countries. The State official's response for Honduras noted that a large percentage of children do not live with their parents, that grandmothers often care for numerous grandchildren, and that domestic violence and sexual abuse are widespread. The USAID official's response for El Salvador

reported a similar dynamic, with children left in the care of non-parents, creating instability or uncertainty for youth who turn to crime, drugs, or migration. The USAID official's response for Honduras noted that such circumstances fuel children's and parent's desire to reunify in the United States.

- Perceptions of U.S. immigration policy: Five agency officials' responses across all three countries identified migrants' perceptions of U.S. immigration policies as a primary cause of UAC migration. For example, the State official's response for Honduras reported that some Hondurans believed that comprehensive immigration reform in the United States would lead to a path to citizenship for anyone living in the United States at the time of reform. The USAID official's response for Honduras reported that some Hondurans believe that unaccompanied children would be reunited with their families and allowed to stay in the United States. Also, as noted above, the State officials' responses for El Salvador and Guatemala noted smugglers spread misinformation about U.S. immigration policies, creating misperceptions among migrants.
- Effects of prior Honduran migration: The USAID and DHS officials' responses for Honduras identified the effects of the global economic crisis compounded by the Honduran political crisis in 2009 and 2010 as a cause of UAC migration. The USAID official's response noted that because of the combined crises large numbers of Hondurans immigrated to the United States and that these migrants now have the means to send for the children they left in Honduras.
- *Mistrust of national police:* The USAID and DHS officials' responses for Honduras identified mistrust of the national police as a cause. The USAID official's response noted that this lack of trust exacerbates the hopelessness many feel regarding violence in their neighborhoods, leading to increased migration.
- *Lack of youth services:* The USAID and DHS officials' responses for Honduras also identified the lack of organizations committed to counseling youth against migration as a cause.

## Agency Officials Reported Little Variance in Causes of Migration by Country

Agency officials' responses showed little variance in causes of migration by country, though, as noted above, three causes were identified only by agency officials responding from Honduras.

- El Salvador: Agency officials did not identify one cause as most responsible for the rapid increase in migration in El Salvador. The State official's response noted the causes are multiple and vary among individuals, but that violence, economic and educational concerns, and the desire for family reunification are the primary drivers. The USAID official's response identified growing violence and crime, including violence and crime due to gang activity, as a primary cause, and noted that gang violence negatively affected economic growth and exacerbated poverty.
- Guatemala: USAID officials identified the lack of economic opportunity, in particular, as the leading cause of UAC migration in Guatemala. The State official's response noted that the Western Highlands of Guatemala and areas around Guatemala City were the main areas of child migration concern, because of poverty in the former, and crime and violence in the latter. Furthermore, the USAID official's response noted poverty in the Western Highlands is also affected by factors other than economic issues, including lack of adequate health services, insufficient access to secondary education and vocational training, and weak governance structures that do not allow for adequate citizen participation. In addition, this response noted that violence caused by organized crime and gangs drove the migration of youth in urban areas such as Guatemala City, while domestic violence was a more prevalent factor in driving youth migration in the Western Highlands. The USAID official's response stated that in certain areas the majority of child migrants are from the middle-class, as the extremely poor cannot afford smugglers' fees.
- Honduras: The DHS official's response stated that violence is the main factor affecting UAC migration. The State and USAID officials' responses reported that most communities from which child migrants come are in low-income, high-violence urban areas, and that economic concerns are likely a greater cause of migration in rural

areas. The State official's response also stated it is believed that smugglers focused their marketing activities on the northern part of the country. Three causes—effects of the prior Honduran migration, mistrust of the national police, and lack of youth services—were identified by agency officials' responses only for Honduras.

## Agency Officials Used a Variety of Sources to Identify Causes of Migration

Agency officials' responses indicated they identified these causes of migration by synthesizing various sources of information, ranging from first-hand discussions with deportees or youth considered to be potential migrants to analyses of literature and statistical data. One or more agency officials' responses reported using the following information sources to identify causes of the rapid increase in migration of unaccompanied children from El Salvador, Guatemala, and Honduras to the United States:

- discussions with deportees, including unaccompanied children, and with migrants' family members;
- USAID-sponsored focus groups composed of youth and community leaders, conducted at various locations in all three countries;
- meetings with host country government officials, civil society organizations, and other stakeholder entities involved in child migration issues;
- intelligence on criminal networks' smuggling efforts;
- homicide data;
- surveys;
- DHS and USAID data on origins of unaccompanied children;
- agency and implementing partner assessments of various sectors and target communities; and
- studies published by various organizations including the United Nations, universities, and USAID contractors.

Officials from all three agencies reported that they had used at least two of the above information sources for corroboration in identifying causes of migration. For example:

- The State official's response for Honduras reported that State identified causes through a combination of surveys, discussions with government agencies and civil society organizations, anecdotal reports, and other sources.
- The USAID official's response for El Salvador reported that USAID corroborated findings resulting from focus group discussions through discussions with host government officials and other stakeholders such as religious leaders. The USAID official's response for El Salvador also noted the focus groups included participants from locations that had been included in a DHS-produced map of the locations of origin of unaccompanied child migrants.
- The DHS official's response for Guatemala reported that DHS identified causes through discussions with government officials, stakeholders, and deported children while also reviewing a number of reports and studies to help shape the assessment.

## Agency Officials Report Developing New Programs and Activities and Modifying Existing Ones to Respond to the Rapid Increase in Unaccompanied Child Migration

State, USAID, and DHS officials in El Salvador, Guatemala, and Honduras reported that they had both developed new programs and modified or shifted the priorities of existing programs to address the rapid increase in UAC migration from each of the three countries. Most State and USAID officials' responses noted that the agencies drew on existing funds, such as by shifting mission resources, in developing or modifying these programs. According to the officials, these programs ranged in location from specific communities or cities to border areas to nationwide or regionwide initiatives.

### New Programs and Activities

State, USAID, and DHS officials reported identifying or developing new programs or activities in all three countries. Agency officials reported that most but not all of these programs are specifically targeted to address causes of the rapid increase in UAC migration, such as crime and violence, lack of economic opportunities, and criminal networks that smuggle unaccompanied children. Some of these programs are still being planned. See table 1 for examples of these programs.[8]

**Table 1. Examples of Three Agencies' New Programs and Activities in Response to the Increase in Unaccompanied Alien Child (UAC) Migration**

| Agency and country | Program description | Program location | Agency-identified cause of migration addressed by program | Funding, as reported by agency |
|---|---|---|---|---|
| State | | | | |
| El Salvador | Improved border inspection program | Along Salvadoran border, particularly blind spots between six primary immigration checkpoints | Agency did not specifically link program to identified cause of migration | $500,000 |
| Guatemala | Public outreach radio campaign | Western Highlands | Misinformation concerning U.S. immigration policy | $10,000 |
| Honduras | Training program for prosecutors and judges | Countrywide | Smuggling networks | $25,000 |
| USAID | | | | |
| El Salvador | Provide rehabilitation services to youth in conflict with the law | To be determined—three of the largest UAC communities of origin | Crime and violence | $1.9 million (estimate) |
| Guatemala | Introduction of coffee rust-resistant seedlings to Western Highlands communities | Western Highlands | Poverty and lack of economic opportunity, specifically addressing spread of coffee rust fungus | Not specified |
| El Salvador, Guatemala, Honduras | Reception and repatriation assistance | Returnee in-processing facilities | Lack of youth services | $7.6 million for the three countries |
| DHS | | | | |
| El Salvador, Guatemala, Honduras | Operation Coyote, targeting criminal organizations | El Salvador, Guatemala, Honduras, Panama | Smuggling networks | Not specified |

| Agency and country | Program description | Program location | Agency-identified cause of migration addressed by program | Funding, as reported by agency |
|---|---|---|---|---|
| | involved in child smuggling | | | |
| El Salvador, Guatemala, Honduras[a] | Dangers of the Journey Campaign to discourage illegal migration of unaccompanied minors | El Salvador, Guatemala, Honduras | Smugglers and misperceptions concerning U.S. immigration policy. | Not specified |

Source: GAO analysis of U.S. Agency for International Development (USAID)-, State, and Department of Homeland Security (DHS)-reported data. | GAO-15-362.

[a] DHS provided this program example in its comments on a draft of this report.

## Modified Programs and Activities

State, USAID, and DHS officials also reported modifying programs or activities in all three countries. As with the new programs discussed above, the agency officials reported that most but not all of these modified programs are intended to address causes of the rapid increase in UAC migration, such as crime and violence, lack of educational opportunities, and misinformation spread by child smuggling networks on migration. See table 2 for examples of these programs.[9]

**Table 2. Examples of Three Agencies' Programs and Activities Modified in Response to the Increase in Unaccompanied Alien Child (UAC) Migration**

| Agency and country | Program description | Program location | Causes of migration addressed by program | Funding, as reported by agency |
|---|---|---|---|---|
| State | | | | |
| El Salvador | Partial funding for Salvadoran government campaign against undocumented immigration and the dangers of the journey north | Countrywide | Misinformation by human smugglers | $140,000 |

**Table 2. (Continued)**

| Agency and country | Program description | Program location | Causes of migration addressed by program | Funding, as reported by agency |
|---|---|---|---|---|
| Guatemala | Municipal policing project | Western Highlands, border region | Crime and violence | $2.2 million; can drawon other funding if needed |
| Honduras | Vetted units and task forces to intercept child migrants and smugglers | All along Honduran border with El Salvador and Guatemala | Smuggling networks | $600,000 |
| USAID | | | | |
| El Salvador | Improve school infrastructure and educational resources | 51 municipalities including those with high numbers of UAC | Crime and violence | $6.1 million |
| Guatemala | Crime prevention programming | Active in high-crime municipalities; would be expanded to Western Highlands communities with rising violence levels | Crime and violence | Not specified |
| Honduras | Improving education for work and learning (program extension) | San Pedro Sula, Tegucigalpa, La Ceiba (three of the largest cities in Honduras) | Lack of educational opportunities | $3 million |
| DHS | | | | |
| El Salvador, Guatemala, Honduras | Transnational criminal investigative units targeted to address smuggling | El Salvador, Guatemala, Honduras, Panama | Smuggling networks | Not specified |
| El Salvador, Guatemala, Honduras[a] | Dangers of the Journey Campaign to discourage illegal migration of | El Salvador, Guatemala, Honduras | Smugglers and misperceptions concerning U.S. | Not specified |

| Agency and country | Program description | Program location | Causes of migration addressed by program | Funding, as reported by agency |
|---|---|---|---|---|
| | unaccompanied minors | | immigration policy. | |

Source: GAO analysis of U.S. Agency for International Development (USAID)-, State, and Department of Homeland Security (DHS)-reported data. | GAO-15-362

[a] DHS provided this program example in its comments on a draft of this report.

State officials in all three countries also reported diplomatic outreach efforts conducted in response to the rapid increase in UAC migration. For example, the State official's response for El Salvador noted that State, USAID, and DHS officials periodically meet with host government officials to coordinate messaging intended to warn Salvadorans about the dangers of the journey to the United States, among other issues. The State official's response for Guatemala noted that high-level visits have played an important role in raising the profile of the UAC issue with the host government. The State official's response for Honduras noted that the embassy modified its diplomatic engagement to focus on this issue and that addressing the UAC issue became the embassy's highest priority in June, July, and August 2014. The response also noted embassy staff met with the highest levels of the Honduran government on at least a weekly basis to focus on this issue and supported weekly visits from congressional delegations and executive branch officials. In addition, in commenting on a draft of this report, State noted that several high-level meetings and trips to the region involving the U.S. President, Vice President, Secretary of State, and other State officials, as well as Salvadoran, Guatemalan, and Honduran government officials, demonstrated that the issue was a priority.

## Pre-existing Programs and Activities

Although State and USAID officials reported developing and modifying programs in response to the rapid increase in UAC migration, these agency officials also noted that their pre-existing efforts and strategic objectives, which had been in place prior to the rapid increase in migration, addressed related issues.

- USAID officials' responses for all three countries noted that the agency's pre-existing programs or strategic objectives focus on causes of the rapid increase in child migration, particularly reducing violence and increasing educational opportunities and economic growth. For example, the USAID official's response for El Salvador noted its recently approved country development cooperation strategy focuses on many issues directly related to the rapid increase in child migration to the United States, with development objectives focusing on reducing violence and economic growth. The USAID official's response for Guatemala also noted that the development objectives of its country development cooperation strategy focus on economic growth and improving social development in the Western Highlands and on increasing security and justice in Guatemala with an emphasis on municipalities that experience high levels of violent crime. For example, in Guatemala, USAID is working to provide alternative basic education opportunities for out-of-school youth in the Western Highlands, and to improve education quality by supporting the Ministry of Education in several areas such as teacher training. Similarly, the USAID official's response for Honduras noted that its principal objectives in its recently approved country development strategy are improving citizen security and reducing extreme poverty.
- The State official's response for El Salvador noted that the department's Partnership for Growth bilateral initiative has, since 2011, sought to address, among other issues, crime and the need for improved education, which State identified as causes of child migration. Similarly, the State official's response for Guatemala noted that the post already had in place programs addressing causes of migration such as violence and poverty. Specifically, the State official's response outlined a number of post efforts intended to increase economic activity in Guatemala, such as by encouraging U.S. businesses to invest in Guatemala and providing assistance to Guatemalan entrepreneurs. In addition, the State official's response outlined post activities to strengthen police and judicial sector entities, which are aimed at reducing violence.

## Planning Efforts

State, USAID, and DHS officials reported that they have undertaken various efforts to plan their responses to the increase in migration, including coordinating among U.S. agencies and with host governments. For example, agency officials for all three countries reported participating in UAC interagency working groups at each embassy. Agency officials reported that these working groups enabled them to share information, discuss strategy, and coordinate the interagency response. In addition, agency officials reported they have taken various steps to assess host country needs related to the rapid increase in migration. For example:

- The State and USAID officials' responses for Honduras noted they had requested information on assistance needs from the First Lady of Honduras, who heads the country's unaccompanied child migration task force.
- The USAID officials' responses for all three countries reported that, to help shape the agency's assistance efforts, it assessed all three host governments' capacity to accept repatriated unaccompanied child migrants.
- The DHS official's response for Guatemala reported that DHS officials in Guatemala hold periodic meetings with host government officials to identify possible needs in areas such as addressing the flow of migrants across the border and combating criminal organizations operating out of the country.

In addition, State and USAID officials said they have used DHS data on the locations of origin of UAC to help inform their identification of the causes of migration or programming decisions, in conjunction with other sources of information. Specifically, the State officials' written responses for Guatemala and Honduras indicate that DHS data on the origins of UAC migrants informed the agency's identification of causes of migration. Moreover, State officials in Washington, D.C., told us that, when they began reprioritizing programs in the summer of 2014 in response to the rapid increase in unaccompanied child migration, they consulted DHS's map on UAC locations of origin to help determine where to locate programs. In addition, the USAID official's response for Honduras referenced DHS's map of UAC by location of origin when discussing the variance of causes of UAC migration across

Honduras. The USAID official's response for Guatemala indicated that the map informed agency efforts to locate new programs.

According to CBP, Border Patrol agents obtain information on UAC origins by interviewing children—or, in some cases, those traveling with them—who have been apprehended at the U.S. border. According to CBP officials, there are various challenges to obtaining UAC location information. These challenges can include the following:

- The children can be so young that they do not know where they are from.
- The children may offer the name of the largest city near where they are from if they are in fact from a small village near the city.
- There can be a language barrier. Not all agents are equally fluent in Spanish. In addition, State noted that agents may not be fluent in the indigenous languages spoken by many UACs, and that UACs may report their community of origin by its indigenous name.
- The children usually do not have documents indicating where they came from.
- Smugglers can coach the children to provide a certain location.

CBP officials indicated that if the child does not know where he or she is from, the agent may enter the child's description of his or her home geography into the database field or simply enter the name of the country. In May and July 2014, DHS's Office of Intelligence and Analysis produced two maps of UAC locations of origin based on data it obtained from CBP. Although the first DHS map produced in May 2014 did not include any caveats about the challenges in obtaining this information, the second map produced in July 2014 included language that noted, among other things, that locations in the data were self-reported.[10] The USAID official's response for Honduras noted that, in Honduras, USAID and DHS are working with the government to improve its intake, analysis, and mapping of returnees' communities of origin.

## AGENCY COMMENTS AND OUR EVALUATION

We are not making any recommendations in this report. We provided State, USAID, DHS, and MCC a draft of this report for advance review and comment. The agencies did not provide written comments. State, USAID, and

DHS provided technical comments, which we have incorporated, as appropriate.

Sincerely yours,

David Gootnick
Director
International Affairs and Trade

## APPENDIX I: OBJECTIVES, SCOPE, AND METHODOLOGY

We examined U.S. mission-level efforts to (1) identify causes of the rapid increase in migration of unaccompanied children and (2) address the causes identified. To address these objectives, we developed a set of questions to obtain written responses from mission heads and other U.S. agency officials responsible for programs in El Salvador, Guatemala, and Honduras about the causes they identified for the rapid increase in unaccompanied child migration and the actions they have taken in these three countries to address those causes. Specifically, we obtained responses reflecting the perspectives of the following agency officials in each of the three countries: the ambassadors, regarding Department of State (State) efforts; the mission directors, regarding U.S. Agency for International Development (USAID) efforts; and the country attachés, regarding Department of Homeland Security (DHS) efforts. These officials had been designated by their respective agencies as appropriate sources of information about programs in their respective countries. We also contacted Millennium Challenge Corporation officials responsible for programs in El Salvador, Guatemala, and Honduras. However, these officials noted that it is not within the corporation's mandate to directly address migration issues and that the corporation has not modified its compact program to address the recent rapid increase in unaccompanied child migration. Therefore, we did not include Millennium Challenge Corporation efforts in this report. This report includes the nine responses from State, USAID, and DHS officials.

We reviewed, analyzed, and tabulated the nine State, USAID, and DHS officials' responses. Specifically, to count the causes agency officials most commonly identified as primarily responsible for the rapid increase in unaccompanied alien child (UAC) migration from El Salvador, Guatemala, and Honduras to the United States, two analysts separately coded and verified all nine agency officials' responses. One analyst first coded all agency officials' responses by type of cause identified. A second analyst then reviewed this coding structure. Any initial disagreements in coding were reconciled between the two analysts. In addition, agency officials reported funding information for some programs developed or modified in response to the rapid increase in UAC migration. However, we did not assess the reliability of the funding data reported by agency officials for this report, and are providing it for background and context only. We also interviewed agency officials in Washington, D.C.

We conducted this performance audit from September 2014 to February 2015 in accordance with generally accepted government auditing standards. Those standards require that we plan and perform the audit to obtain sufficient, appropriate evidence to provide a reasonable basis for our findings and conclusions based on our audit objectives. We believe that the evidence obtained provides a reasonable basis for our findings.

## End Notes

[1] U.S. law defines an unaccompanied alien child, or UAC, as "a child who has no lawful immigration status in the United States; has not attained 18 years of age; and with respect to whom there is no parent or legal guardian in the United States or no parent or legal guardian in the United States available to provide care and physical custody." 6 U.S.C. § 279(g)(2).

[2] A compact is a multiyear agreement between the Millennium Challenge Corporation and an eligible country to fund specific programs targeted at reducing poverty and stimulating economic growth. The corporation's threshold program is designed to assist countries that have not yet qualified for compact assistance but have demonstrated a significant commitment to improving their performance on the corporation's eligibility criteria.

[3] We also contacted the Millennium Challenge Corporation about its programs in El Salvador, Guatemala, and Honduras. Millennium Challenge Corporation officials' noted that the corporation's recently signed compact with El Salvador and proposed threshold program with Guatemala may address some causes of migration such as lack of economic and educational opportunities. However, these officials noted that it is not within the corporation's mandate to directly address migration issues and that the corporation has not modified its compact program to address the recent rapid increase in unaccompanied child migration. Therefore, we did not include Millennium Challenge Corporation efforts in the body of this report.

[4] Plan of the Alliance for Prosperity in the Northern Triangle: A Road Map. Regional Plan Prepared by El Salvador, Guatemala, and Honduras. September 2014.

[5] The Corruption Perception Index ranks countries around the world according to the degree of corruption that is perceived to exist among public officials and politicians on an annual basis. A lower ranking means a higher degree of corruption is perceived to exist.

[6] GAO, Central America: U.S. Agencies Considered Various Factors in Funding Security Activities, but Need to Assess Progress in Achieving Interagency Objectives, GAO-13-771 (Washington, D.C.: Sept. 25, 2013).

[7] Coffee is a leading export in Guatemala and Honduras.

[8] We selected the programs included in table 1 from a larger list for purposes of illustrating different types of new programs that address different causes, which agency officials reported.

[9] We selected the programs included in table 2 from a larger list for purposes of illustrating different types of modified programs that address different causes, which agency officials reported.

[10] We plan to further analyze agencies' use of UAC location of origin data and other information as it informs assistance targeting and performance evaluation, and we will report on the results of our analysis later this year.

In: Unaccompanied Children from Central America ISBN: 978-1-63482-937-3
Editor: Veronica K. Quinn 

*Chapter 2*

# UNACCOMPANIED ALIEN CHILDREN: DEMOGRAPHICS IN BRIEF*

***Ruth Ellen Wasem and Austin Morris***

## SUMMARY

The number of children coming to the United States who are not accompanied by parents or legal guardians and who lack proper immigration documents has raised complex and competing sets of humanitarian concerns and immigration control issues. This report focuses on the demographics of unaccompanied alien children while they are in removal proceedings. Overwhelmingly, the children are coming from El Salvador, Guatemala, and Honduras. The median age of unaccompanied children has decreased from 17 years in FY2011 to 16 years during the first seven months of FY2014. A greater share of males than females are represented among this population. However, females have steadily increased in total numbers and as a percentage of the flow since FY2011. The median age of females has dropped from 17 years in FY2011—the year that was the median age across all groups of children—to 15 years in the first seven months of FY2014.

* This is an edited, reformatted and augmented version of a Congressional Research Service publication R43734, prepared for Members and Committees of Congress, dated September 24, 2014.

# INTRODUCTION

The sheer number of children coming to the United States who are not accompanied by parents or legal guardians has raised considerable concern.[1] Overwhelmingly, the children are coming from El Salvador, Guatemala, and Honduras. This report focuses on the demographics of unaccompanied alien children[2] while they are in removal proceedings.[3] It discusses the characteristics of these children by nationality, age, and sex and explores these trends over the past few years. It further builds on a set of Congressional Research Service (CRS) reports examining the issues surrounding unaccompanied alien children.[4]

**Definition of "Unaccompanied Alien Child"**

The statutory definition of an "unaccompanied alien child" is a child who has no lawful immigration status in the United States; has not attained 18 years of age; and with respect to whom—there is no parent or legal guardian in the United States; or no parent or legal guardian in the United States is available to provide care and physical custody. [6 U.S.C. §279(g)(2).]

## Office of Refugee Resettlement Data on Unaccompanied Alien Children

After Customs and Border Protection (CBP)[5] agents in the Department of Homeland Security (DHS) have apprehended and processed an unaccompanied alien child,[6] DHS transfers the child into the custody of the Department of Health and Human Services' (HHS's) Office of Refugee Resettlement (ORR).[7] ORR is responsible for placing unaccompanied alien children in appropriate care. The law requires that ORR ensure that the interests of the child are considered in decisions and actions relating to the care and custody of an unaccompanied child.[8] ORR also oversees the infrastructure and personnel of residential facilities for unaccompanied alien children, among other responsibilities. ORR arranges to house the unaccompanied child either in one of its shelters or in a foster care arrangement, or it reunites the unaccompanied child with a family member.

In this report, the demographic and placement trends of unaccompanied children are based upon summary data extracted from case file data that ORR maintains on unaccompanied alien children.[9] Due to the confidential nature of ORR data generally, CRS used only selected variables for this analysis.[10] The summary data span the period between FY2011 and FY2014.[11] The FY2014 data are partial (available through April 30, 2014), which made it difficult to reach conclusions about patterns or trends when comparing to the other three fiscal years.

# DEMOGRAPHICS OF UNACCOMPANIED CHILDREN

## Country of Origin

Much attention has been focused on the top countries of origin for the unaccompanied children. Over the past four years, ORR had unaccompanied children in its custody from 87 different countries, ranging from 41 to 50 different countries each fiscal year. Nevertheless, El Salvador, Guatemala, and Honduras have consistently accounted for the overwhelming majority of all unaccompanied children in ORR custody (*Table 1*).

**Table 1. Unaccompanied Children in ORR Custody by Top Country October 1, 2010, to April 30, 2014**

| | Honduras | Guatemala | El Salvador | All Others |
|---|---|---|---|---|
| FY2011 | 848 | 1,414 | 1,142 | 1,481 |
| FY2012 | 3,692 | 4,842 | 3,806 | 1,992 |
| FY2013 | 7,028 | 8,381 | 6,054 | 1,859 |
| FY2014* | 9,157 | 8,908 | 6,425 | 1,444 |

Source: CRS analysis of summary data from unpublished ORR data on unaccompanied alien children.

Note: FY2014 accounts for data only through April 30, 2014, representing seven months of a full fiscal year.

While the most notable increase in unaccompanied children over the past three fiscal years and the first seven months of FY2014 was from Honduras (980%)—as it steadily increased in overall rank from fourth in FY2011 to first through the first seven months of FY2014—even the smallest increase in unaccompanied children in ORR custody of the three countries (El Salvador) was notable: 463% from FY2011 through the first seven months of FY2014 (*Figure 1*).

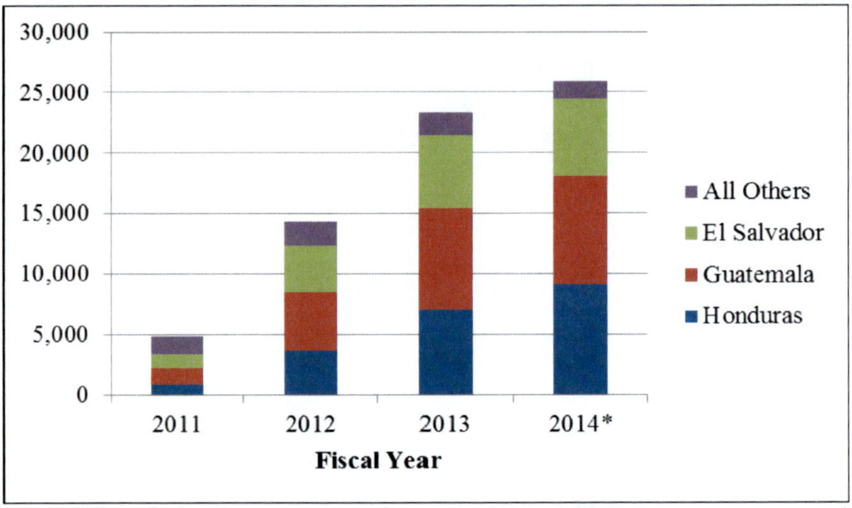


Source: CRS analysis of summary data from unpublished ORR data on unaccompanied alien children.

Note: FY2014 accounts for data only through April 30, 2014, representing seven months of a full fiscal year.

Figure 1. Unaccompanied Children in ORR Custody by Top Country Distribution. (October 1, 2010, to April 30, 2014)

Not all apprehended unaccompanied children are transferred to ORR, as some are voluntarily returned to their home countries. Although Mexican children generally make up a sizeable number of the unaccompanied alien children apprehended by CBP officers, only a portion of them end up in ORR custody. For example, CBP apprehended 11,577 Mexican unaccompanied children in the first eight months of FY2014,[12] and only 494 Mexican unaccompanied children were placed in ORR custody during the first seven months of FY2014.[13]

## Age

Age is a key factor to qualify as an unaccompanied alien child under the law. The Homeland Security Act of 2002 defines an unaccompanied alien child as an individual who has no lawful immigration status in the United

States, has not yet reached the age of 18, and has no parent or legal guardian in the United States or no parent or legal guardian in the United States who is available to provide care and physical custody.[14] Those 18 and older in ORR custody could have entered the United States shortly before turning 18, could be awaiting transfer back to DHS custody, or could have special needs[15] that have kept them in ORR custody past the age of 18.

**Table 2. Unaccompanied Children in ORR Custody by Age Group October 1, 2010, to April 30, 2014**

| | Median Age | 0-9 years | 10-12 years | 13-15 years | 16-17 years | 18 years | 19+ years |
|---|---|---|---|---|---|---|---|
| FY2011 | 17 years | 175 | 179 | 556 | 1,819 | 1,870 | 286 |
| FY2012 | 17 years | 430 | 706 | 2,502 | 7,063 | 3,412 | 221 |
| FY2013 | 16 years | 1,169 | 1,717 | 5,504 | 12,857 | 1,800 | 278 |
| FY2014* | 16 years | 1,803 | 2,700 | 6,501 | 11,872 | 2,925 | 133 |

Source: CRS analysis of summary data from unpublished ORR data on unaccompanied alien children. Note: FY2014 accounts for data only through April 30, 2014, representing 7 months of a full fiscal year.

The median age of unaccompanied children in ORR custody was 17 years old in FY2011 and FY2012, as *Table 2* presents. The median age fell to 16 years old in FY2013 and has remained there in the first seven months of FY2014. The youngest three age groups (0-9, 10-12, and 13-15 years old) experienced the most percentage growth compared to the oldest three age groups (16- 17, 18, and 19+ years old), which have experienced a percentage decrease during the period examined (*Figure 2*). While there continued to be a greater overall number of older children in ORR custody, there was also a noteworthy increase in younger children in ORR custody, particularly in the 10-12 age group (*Figure 2*) over the period studied. From October 1, 2010, through April 30, 2014, ORR had a total of 8,879 unaccompanied children under the age of 13 in its custody.

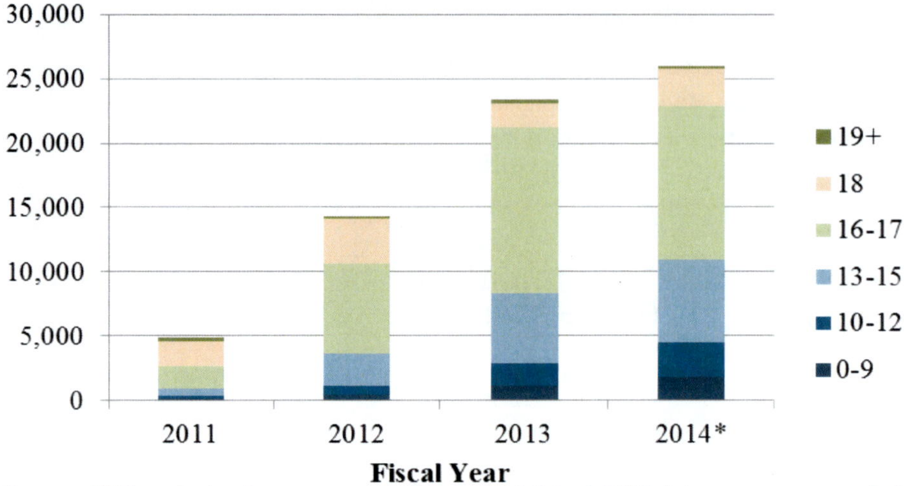


Source: CRS analysis of summary data from unpublished ORR data on unaccompanied alien children.

Note: FY2014 accounts for data only through April 30, 2014, representing seven months of a full fiscal year.

Figure 2. Age Distribution of Unaccompanied Children in ORR Custody. (October 1, 2010, to April 30, 2014)

## Nationality and Age Distribution

From FY2011 through the first seven months of FY2014, there was an increase in the number of children in each of the three youngest age brackets (0-9, 10-12, and 13-15) for Honduras, Guatemala, and El Salvador. Most notably, in the first seven months of FY2014, the youngest three age brackets for Honduras made up over half of all Honduran unaccompanied children (6,242). Like Honduras and El Salvador, Guatemala had an increase in the three youngest age brackets, however, it also had the greatest number of unaccompanied children in the oldest three age brackets (16-17, 18, and 19+) (*Figure 3*).

## Sex

Traditionally there have been more male than female unaccompanied children in ORR custody. In 2002, immigration officials testified that the overwhelming majority of unaccompanied alien children were male.[16] The number of unaccompanied females increased from 1,075 in FY2011 to 5,385 in FY2013. The number of unaccompanied girls reached 2,959 in the first seven months of FY2014. Similarly, the percentage of females among unaccompanied children has grown. The share of females was stable at about 22% in FY2011 and FY2012 and increased to about 27% in FY2013 and 33% in the first seven months of FY2014 (*Figure 4*).

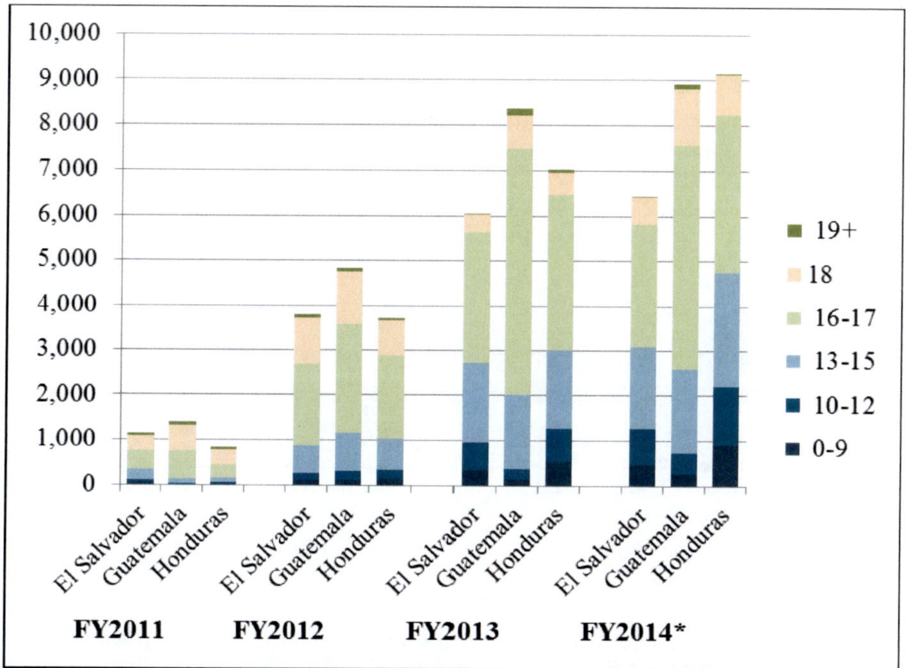


Source: CRS analysis of summary data from unpublished ORR data on unaccompanied alien children.

Note: FY2014 accounts for data only through April 30, 2014, representing seven months of a full fiscal year.

Figure 3. Unaccompanied Children in ORR Custody by Nationality and Age. (October 1, 2010, to April 30, 2014)

As previously shown in *Figure 1*, the overwhelming majority of unaccompanied children in ORR custody from FY2011 through the first seven months of FY2014 originated from Honduras, Guatemala, and El Salvador. The sex distribution from the top countries of origin among children in ORR custody was examined to provide a better understanding of the female population. Examining the male-to-female ratio for each specific top source country reveals that a greater proportion of females in ORR custody originated from El Salvador than from Honduras, while a lower proportion of females originated from Guatemala (*Figure 5)*. Honduras had the most females in ORR custody and was also the country with the greatest number of minors in ORR custody overall.

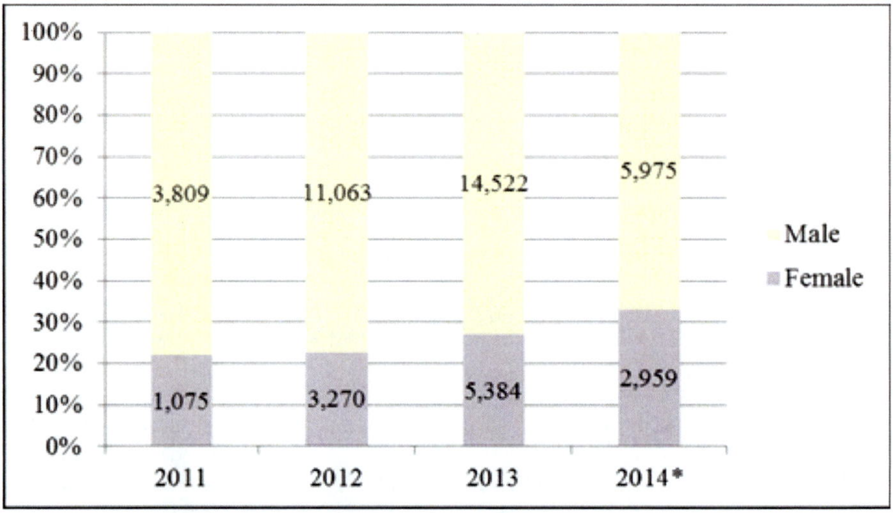


Source: CRS analysis of summary data from unpublished ORR data on unaccompanied alien children.

Note: FY2014 accounts for data only through April 30, 2014, representing seven months of a full fiscal year.

Figure 4. Sex Distribution of Unaccompanied Children in ORR Custody. (October 1, 2010, to April 30, 2014)

In absolute numbers, most males in ORR custody were ages 16-17 in each of the three fiscal years and in the first seven months of FY2014; however, the number of males age 0-9, 10-12, and 13-15 steadily increased over the past three fiscal years and in the first seven months of FY2014 (*Figure 6*). Similar patterns occurred for females. In the first seven months of FY2014, the number of females in the 16-17 age bracket increased, whereas the number of males decreased (*Figure 7*).

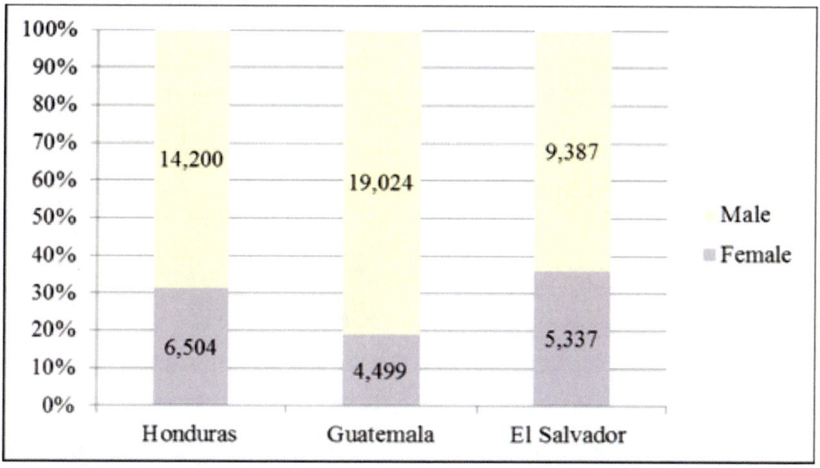


Source: CRS analysis of summary data from unpublished ORR data on unaccompanied alien children.

Note: FY2014 accounts for data only through April 30, 2014, representing seven months of a full fiscal year.

Figure 5. Sex Distribution of Unaccompanied Children by Top Countries. (October 1, 2010, to April 30, 2014)

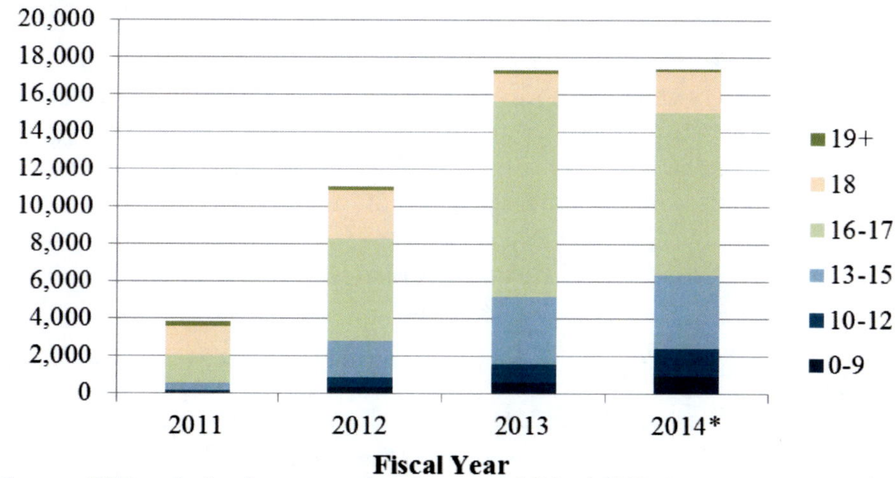


Source: CRS analysis of summary data from unpublished ORR data on unaccompanied alien children.

Note: FY2014 accounts for data only through April 30, 2014, representing seven months of a full fiscal year.

Figure 6. Age Distribution for Unaccompanied Males. (October 1, 2010, to April 30, 2014)

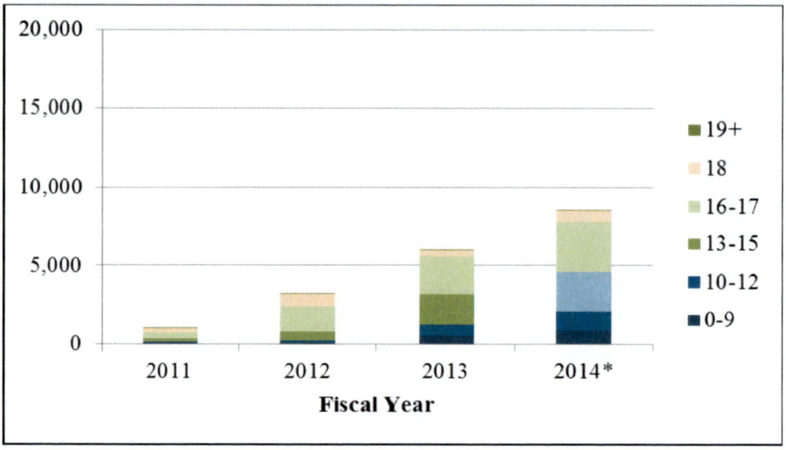


Source: CRS analysis of summary data from unpublished ORR data on unaccompanied alien children.

Note: FY2014 accounts for data only through April 30, 2014, representing seven months of a full fiscal year.

Figure 7. Age Distribution for Unaccompanied Females. (October 1, 2010, to April 30, 2014)

The median age of unaccompanied children by year, sex, and top country (*Table 3*) present the age trends a bit more starkly. The median age of females has dropped from 17 years in FY2011— the year that was the median age across all groups of children—to 15 years in the first seven months of FY2014. The median age for females in FY2013 was 13 years. When viewed by country, the median age decreased for all three and fell to 15 years for Honduran children during the first seven months of FY2014.

**Table 3. Median Age of Unaccompanied Children by Year, Sex, and Top Country**

| | Sex | | Top Countries | | |
|---|---|---|---|---|---|
| Year | Male | Female | Guatemala | Honduras | El Salvador |
| FY2011 | 17 | 17 | 17 | 17 | 17 |
| FY2012 | 17 | 16 | 17 | 17 | 16 |
| FY2013 | 17 | 13 | 16 | 16 | 16 |
| FY2014* | 16 | 15 | 16 | 15 | 16 |

Source: CRS analysis of summary data from unpublished ORR data on unaccompanied alien children.

Notes: FY2014 accounts for data only through April 30, 2014, representing seven months of a full fiscal year.

# End Notes

[1] During the first eight months of FY2014, the Office of Refugee Resettlement (ORR) had over 38,000 unaccompanied alien children in custody. For further information, see CRS Report R43599, Unaccompanied Alien Children: An Overview, by Lisa Seghetti, Alison Siskin, and Ruth Ellen Wasem.

[2] This report uses the terms "unaccompanied alien children," "UAC," and "unaccompanied children" interchangeably.

[3] For basics on the Executive Office for Immigration Review (EOIR) immigration courts and removal proceedings, see U.S. Department of Justice, Executive Office for Immigration Review, EOIR at a Glance, September 9, 2010, http://www.justice.gov/eoir/press/2010/EOIRataGlance09092010.htm. For an evaluation of EOIR's performance, see U.S. Department of Justice, Office of the Inspector General, Management of Immigration Cases and Appeals by the Executive Office for Immigration Review, October 2012, http://www.justice.gov/oig/reports/2012/e1301.pdf.

[4] CRS Report R43599, Unaccompanied Alien Children: An Overview, by Lisa Seghetti, Alison Siskin, and Ruth Ellen Wasem; CRS Report IN10107, Unaccompanied Alien Children: A Processing Flow Chart, by Lisa Seghetti; CRS Report R43628, Unaccompanied Alien Children: Potential Factors Contributing to Recent Immigration, coordinated by William A. Kandel; CRS Report R43623, Unaccompanied Alien Children—Legal Issues: Answers to Frequently Asked Questions, by Kate M. Manuel and Michael John Garcia; CRS Report R43664, Asylum Policies for Unaccompanied Children Compared with Expedited Removal Policies for Unauthorized Adults: In Brief, by Ruth Ellen Wasem; and CRS Report R41731, Central America Regional Security Initiative: Background and Policy Issues for Congress, by Peter J. Meyer and Clare Ribando Seelke.

[5] Customs and Border Protection (CBP) is one of the U.S. Department of Homeland Security agencies charged with the enforcement of immigration laws. Its two major arms for immigration activities are the U.S. Border Patrol, which is responsible for enforcing immigration law between ports of entry, and the Office of Field Operations (OFO) which is responsible for conducting immigration inspections at the ports of entry.

[6] CBP also issues "Notices to Appear" (NTAs) for removal proceedings.

[7] Not all apprehended unaccompanied children are transferred to ORR, as some are voluntarily returned to their home countries.

[8] §235(c) of the Trafficking Victims Protection Reauthorization Act and §462(b) of the Homeland Security Act of 2002 (P.L. 107-296) describe conditions for the care and placement of unaccompanied alien children in federal custody.

[9] These data are not published; ORR released the data to CRS pursuant to a CRS request.

[10] Those variables that might identify the children or the families have been excluded from the summary files. Therefore, only the age, gender, country of birth, type of discharge, and relationship to the minor are included in the summary files.

[11] FY2014 accounts for data only from October 1, 2013, through April 30, 2014.

[12] CBP released FY2014 data through May 31, 2014.

[13] CBP personnel screen unaccompanied children to determine that the child has not been a victim of a severe form of trafficking in persons and that there is no credible evidence that the minor is at risk if returned to the country of nationality or of last habitual residence, that the child does not have a possible claim to asylum, and that the child is able to make an independent decision to voluntarily return to his or her country of nationality or of last habitual residence. As a result of the initial screening, a greater proportion of Mexican

children are returned to Mexico and not transferred to ORR custody compared with unaccompanied minors from non-contiguous countries. See CRS Report R43599, Unaccompanied Alien Children: An Overview, by Lisa Seghetti, Alison Siskin, and Ruth Ellen Wasem.

[14] Homeland Security Act of 2002, §462.

[15] Unaccompanied children with special needs are those who have medical and psychological needs. For further discussion, see University of Texas at El Paso, National Center for Border Security and Immigration, Unaccompanied Alien Children (UAC) Project, March 20, 2014, pp. 11-24, http://ncbsi.utep.edu/documents/ UAC%20Project% 20Site% 20Visits/UTEP%20NCBSI%20Final%20Report%20March%2020%202014.pdf.

[16] U.S. Congress, Senate Committee on the Judiciary, The Unaccompanied Alien Child Protection Act, hearing 107th Cong., 2nd sess., February 28, 2002, p. 38.

In: Unaccompanied Children from Central America ISBN: 978-1-63482-937-3
Editor: Veronica K. Quinn 

*Chapter 3*

# UNACCOMPANIED CHILDREN FROM CENTRAL AMERICA: FOREIGN POLICY CONSIDERATIONS*

***Peter J. Meyer, Clare Ribando Seelke, Maureen Taft-Morales and Rhoda Margesson***

## SUMMARY

In FY2014, there was a sharp increase in the number of unaccompanied alien children (UAC) traveling to the United States. U.S. authorities apprehended more than 68,500 unaccompanied minors at the U.S. border in FY2014, 75% of whom came from El Salvador, Guatemala, and Honduras—the "northern triangle" of Central America. This unexpected surge of children strained U.S. government resources and created a complex crisis with humanitarian implications for the United States and the international community. Although the flow of unaccompanied minors has slowed since peaking in June 2014, experts warn that it will likely accelerate again in the future unless policy makers in the countries of origin and the international community take steps to address the poor socioeconomic and security conditions driving Central Americans to leave their homes.

---

* This is an edited, reformatted and augmented version of a Congressional Research Service publication R43702, prepared for Members and Committees of Congress, dated February 10, 2015.

The 2014 crisis led to renewed focus on Central America, a region with which the United States historically has shared close political, economic, and cultural ties. The United States currently engages with Central American countries through a variety of mechanisms, including the Dominican Republic-Central America-United States Free Trade Agreement (CAFTA-DR) and several foreign assistance programs. Over the past year, the Obama Administration has sought closer cooperation with Central American governments to dissuade children from making the journey to the United States, target smuggling networks, and repatriate unauthorized migrants.

Asserting that the FY2014 surge in unaccompanied minors was a reminder that "the security and prosperity of Central America are inextricably linked to our own," the Administration has requested $1 billion in foreign assistance for the region in FY2016. These funds would be used to implement a new "U.S. Strategy for Engagement in Central America," a whole-of-government approach designed to increase economic opportunity, reduce extreme violence, and strengthen the effectiveness of state institutions in Central America. The request would allow existing programs to be scaled up significantly and would place greater emphasis on economic prosperity and governance while continuing to address security concerns in the region.

The 113$^{th}$ Congress expressed considerable concern about the spike in apprehensions of unaccompanied children from Central America, with Members holding numerous hearings, traveling to the region, and introducing legislation. Although Congress opted not to appropriate supplemental funding for programs in Central America in FY2014, it included additional resources for the region in its FY2015 appropriations measure (P.L. 113-235). Congress also directed the Administration to develop a comprehensive strategy to address the key factors contributing to the migration of unaccompanied children to the United States.

The 114$^{th}$ Congress will continue to shape U.S. policy toward Central America. It will consider the Administration's $1 billion FY2016 request for the region and will review the strategy required by P.L. 113-235. Congress also may consider other measures, such as H.R. 439 (Weber) and H.R. 530 (Burgess), which, respectively, would suspend and reduce foreign assistance to El Salvador, Guatemala, Honduras, and Mexico if those countries proved unwilling or unable to prevent unauthorized migration to the United States.

As Congress continues to debate legislative options to address the foreign policy dimensions of the situation, there are a variety of interrelated issues that it might take into consideration. These might include Central American governments' limited capacities to receive and reintegrate repatriated children, and their abilities and willingness to address the pervasive insecurity and lack of socioeconomic opportunities in their countries that cause many children to leave. Other issues

Congress might consider include the extent to which the Mexican government is capable of limiting the transmigration of Central Americans through its territory and how international humanitarian actors are responding to the situation in Central America.

## INTRODUCTION

In FY2014, there was a sharp increase in the number of unaccompanied children[1] traveling to the United States. U.S. Customs and Border Patrol (CBP) apprehended more than 68,500 unaccompanied minors—a 77% increase compared to FY2013. This dramatic spike strained U.S. government resources, created a complex crisis with humanitarian implications, and raised concerns both domestically and internationally about the safety and protection of the children.

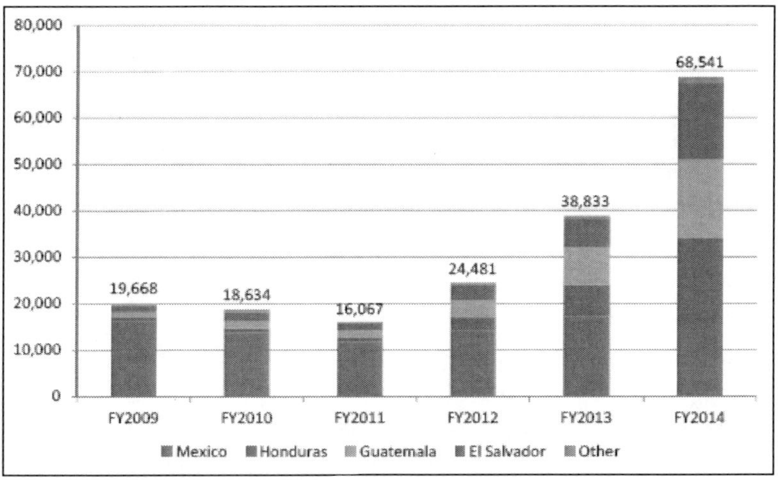


Source: U.S. Border Patrol, "Unaccompanied Children (Age 0-17) Apprehensions, Fiscal Year 2008 through Fiscal Year 2012," February 4, 2013; and U.S. Customs and Border Protection, "Southwest Border Unaccompanied Alien Children (FY 2014)" press release, October 2014.

Figure 1.Apprehensions of Unaccompanied Minors by Country of Origin: FY2009-FY2014.

The changing demographics of the unaccompanied minors apprehended at the border contributed to the complexity of the situation. Whereas the vast majority of unaccompanied minors came from Mexico prior to FY2012, the

FY2014 surge was attributable to children from the countries from the so-called "northern triangle" of Central America—El Salvador, Guatemala, and Honduras (see *Figure 1*)—who are subject to a different administrative process under U.S. law.[2] Moreover, there were considerable increases in the numbers of young children and female minors arriving at the U.S. border. While the bulk of the unaccompanied minors that were apprehended were teenage boys, the proportion of children that were 12 or younger increased from 9% in FY2013 to 16% in FY2014, and the proportion that were girls increased from 19% in FY2013 to 28% in FY2014.[3]

There is little consensus among analysts regarding why this sharp increase occurred in FY2014. However, most maintain that the problem is complex, involving interactions between so-called "push factors," such as high levels of violence and poverty in Central America, and "pull factors," such as the desire to join family members in the United States and perceptions about U.S. immigration policies.[4] Given the diversity of the unaccompanied children and their motives, the lines of distinction between and among refugees, asylum seekers, and migrants are not always clear. Appropriately identifying the individuals or groups at risk is a key challenge for the United States and the international community.

Since peaking in June 2014, the flow of unaccompanied minors has slowed significantly. Just over 10,100 unaccompanied minors were apprehended at the southwest border during the first four months of FY2015, a 39% decline compared to the same period in FY2014.[5] Nevertheless, many analysts warn that the flow is likely to accelerate in the future unless policy makers in the countries of origin and the international community take steps to address the root causes leading Central Americans to abandon their homes.[6]

Members of Congress have expressed significant concerns about the influx of unaccompanied minors and have taken some steps designed to address the situation. This report focuses on the foreign policy dimensions of the crisis.[7] It begins by examining U.S. policy in Central America, including a brief historical background, the current policy framework, and the initial response to the surge in unaccompanied minors. The report then discusses a variety of issues Congress might take into consideration as it formulates policy toward the region. These include the capacity of Central American nations to receive and reintegrate unaccompanied children removed ("deported") from the United States, the capacity of Central American nations to address the root causes of the exodus, the role of Mexico as a transit country, and the response of the international community. The report concludes with an outlook for U.S. policy.

## U.S. POLICY IN CENTRAL AMERICA

The surge in unaccompanied children arriving at the U.S.-Mexico border in 2014 led to a renewed focus on Central America. As Members of Congress debate potential changes in policy toward Central America, they might consider how U.S. policy has influenced the region in the past, the current framework for U.S. engagement in the region, and what steps have been taken thus far to address this most recent migration crisis.

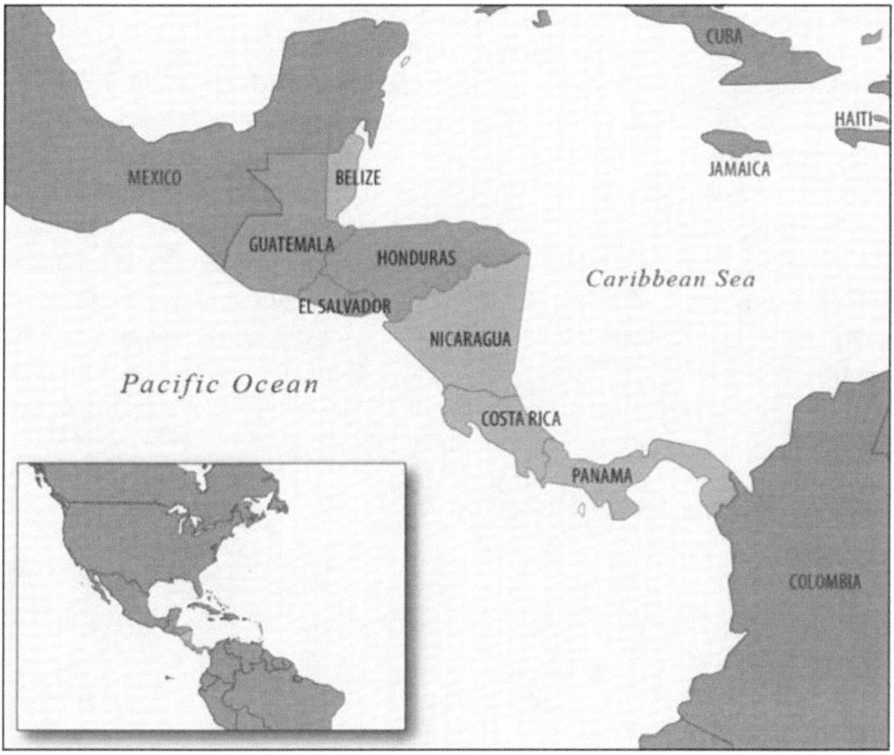


Source: Prepared by Amber Hope Wilhelm, CRS Graphics Specialist.

Notes: El Salvador, Guatemala, and Honduras are often referred to as the "northern triangle" countries.

Figure 2. Map of Central America.

## Background

Given the geographic proximity of Central America, the United States historically has had close political, economic, and cultural ties with the region. During the Cold War, the U.S. government viewed links between the Soviet Union and leftist and nationalist political movements in Central America as a potential threat to U.S. strategic interests. The United States provided extensive assistance (equivalent to $9 billion constant 2012 dollars) to El Salvador, Guatemala, and Honduras during the 1980s as the Salvadoran and Guatemalan governments fought leftist insurgencies and the Honduran government supported U.S. policy in the region.[8] An estimated 70,000 Salvadorans and 200,000 Guatemalans were killed or disappeared during the countries' civil conflicts, and truth commissions have determined that government forces were responsible for the vast majority of human rights abuses committed.[9] Many Central Americans fled the region and sought refuge in the United States. The vast majority of Salvadorans and Guatemalans were denied asylum, however, since the U.S. government insisted that its allies in the region were not responsible for human rights violations.[10] During this time period, the United States established the Caribbean Basin Initiative (CBI, formally the Caribbean Basin Economic Recovery Act). The unilateral preferential trade arrangement, launched in 1983, provided duty-free access to the U.S. market for many goods from the region.

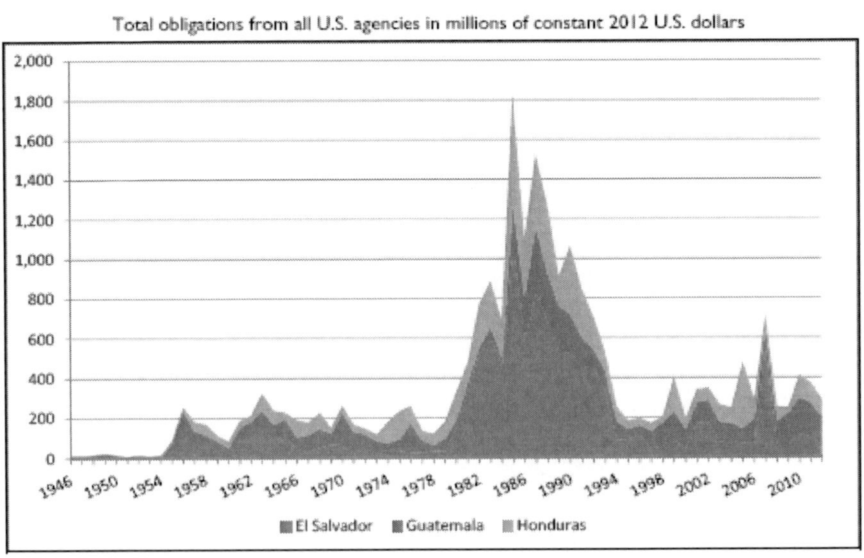

Source: U.S. Agency for International Development (USAID), U.S. Overseas Loans and Grants: Obligations and Loan Authorizations, July 1, 1945-September 30, 2012, http://gbk. eads. usaidallnet.gov/.

Figure 3. U.S. Assistance to El Salvador, Guatemala, and Honduras: FY1946-FY2012.

U.S. support for Central America began to wane in the 1990s following the dissolution of the Soviet Union and the end of the region's civil conflicts. Peace accords were signed in El Salvador in 1992 and in Guatemala in 1996. Although the United States provided some support to Central American countries to strengthen democratic governance and implement market-oriented economic reforms and provided considerable assistance in the aftermath of natural disasters such as Hurricane Mitch in 1998, aid to the northern triangle countries declined significantly during the 1990s (see *Figure 3*). Following the passage of the Illegal Immigrant Reform and Immigrant Responsibility Act (IIRIRA) of 1996, the United States accelerated deportations of Central Americans. Nearly 46,000 convicts were among those deported to the region between 1998 and 2005;[11] these included members of the Mara Salvatrucha (MS-13) and 18th Street Gang (M-18)— both of which were founded in Los Angeles—contributing to the spread of gang violence in Central America.[12]

## Current Policy Framework

The Obama Administration has set forth a broad framework for U.S. policy toward Latin America that includes four principal objectives: promoting economic and social opportunity, ensuring citizen security, strengthening effective institutions of democratic governance, and securing a clean energy future. These policy priorities are based on the premise that "the United States has a vital interest in contributing to the building of stable, prosperous, and democratic nations" in the hemisphere.[13] The U.S. government has sought to advance these priorities in Central America through a variety of mechanisms, including foreign assistance and trade agreements.

Given that El Salvador, Guatemala, and Honduras continue to struggle with major development challenges, foreign aid continues to play a prominent role in U.S. engagement with the region. In FY2014, bilateral assistance provided through the State Department and U.S. Agency for International Development (USAID) totaled an estimated $21.6 million in El Salvador, $65.2 million in Guatemala, and $41.8 million in Honduras (see *Table 1*). This funding was split between efforts to strengthen justice and security sector institutions and traditional development activities in areas such as agriculture, basic education, and economic reform. Although El Salvador received lower levels of aid than its neighbors, it benefited from closer collaboration with the United States through the Partnership for Growth.[14]

The northern triangle countries also benefit from USAID's Central America Regional program, which funds development programs throughout Central America. It supports regional economic harmonization and integration through efforts to facilitate trade and reduce business costs. It also carries out health programs under the President's Emergency Plan for AIDS Relief (PEPFAR) and supports regional collaboration on security issues through the Central American Integration System (SICA). Funding for the regional program was an estimated $33.5 million in FY2014.

**Table 1. U.S. Assistance to Central America: FY2013-FY2015**

Appropriations in millions of current U.S. dollars

| | *FY2013* | *FY2014 (estimate)* | *FY2015 (request)* | *P.L. 113-235 (estimate)*[a] |
|---|---|---|---|---|
| El Salvador | 27.6 | 21.6 | 27.6 | 27.6 |
| Guatemala | 80.8 | 65.2 | 77.1 | 77.1 |
| Honduras | 52.0 | 41.8 | 48.2 | 48.2 |
| Other Central American Countries[b] | 14.7 | 14.4 | 14.8 | NA |
| USAID Central America Regional[c] | 33.1 | 33.5 | 32.0 | NA |
| Central America Regional Security Initiative (CARSI)[c] | 145.6 | 161.5 | 130.0 | 260.0 |
| *Total* | *353.8* | *338.1* | *329.7* | *412.9* |

Source: U.S. Department of State, Congressional Budget Justification for Foreign Operations, Appendix 3: Regional Perspectives, Fiscal Year 2015, April 2014; Explanatory statement accompanying P.L. 113-235; and U.S. Department of State, Congressional Budget Justification: Department of State, Foreign Operations, and Related Programs, Fiscal Year 2016, February 2, 2015.

Notes: These figures only include assistance that is managed by the State Department and USAID. These countries may receive additional assistance from other U.S. agencies.

[a] Estimates based on CRS analysis of the explanatory statement accompanying the Consolidated and Further Continuing Appropriations Act, 2015 (P.L. 113-235). The act did not specify appropriations levels for the other Central American countries or USAID's Central America Regional program.

[b] Includes assistance for Belize, Costa Rica, Nicaragua, and Panama.

[c] It is unclear how much of the funding appropriated for USAID's Central America Regional Program and CARSI will go to each Central American country.

U.S. security cooperation with the countries of the northern triangle has grown considerably in recent years in response to high levels of crime and violence and the region's emergence as a major transit point for illicit narcotics destined for the United States. Much of this cooperation has taken place under the umbrella of the Central America Regional Security Initiative (CARSI).[15] ınitially established in FY2008 as part of the Mexico-focused Mérida Initiative, CARSI provides partner nations with equipment, technical assistance, and training to improve narcotics interdiction and disrupt criminal networks. It also supports Central American law enforcement and justice sector institutions, identifying deficiencies and strengthening their capacities to provide security for the citizens of the region. In addition, CARSI supports crime and violence prevention efforts that seek to reduce drug demand and provide at-risk youth with educational, vocational, and recreational opportunities. In FY2014, CARSI funding totaled an estimated $161.5 million, the majority of which was likely allocated to El Salvador, Guatemala, and Honduras.[16]

The Millennium Challenge Corporation (MCC) provides additional aid to Central American countries.[17] Established in 2004, the MCC awards economic assistance through a competitive selection process to developing nations that demonstrate a commitment to good governance, economic freedom, and investments in their citizens. In 2005, the MCC signed a five-year $205 million[18] compact to improve transportation infrastructure and support rural development in Honduras. Although the MCC Board decided not to renew the compact as a result of the Honduran government's poor performance on corruption, it approved a so-called "threshold program" of up to $15.6 million in 2013 to support Honduran government efforts to strengthen public financial management and increase the transparency and efficiency of public-private partnerships. In 2006, the MCC signed a five-year $461 million compact to support development in the northern border region of El Salvador. A second five-year compact, finalized in September 2014, will provide $277 million to El Salvador to improve the country's investment climate, human capital, and infrastructure.[19] Although Guatemala has yet to receive a compact, the MCC Board approved a $28 million threshold program for the country in December 2014. The program is designed to support fiscal reform, foster partnerships with the private sector, and improve linkages between the education system and the labor market.[20]

Trade and investment relations between the United States and the northern triangle countries are governed by the Dominican Republic-Central America-United States Free Trade Agreement (CAFTA-DR), which was signed in 2004 and entered into force for El Salvador, Guatemala, and Honduras in 2006. The agreement builds on CBI by making preferential market access reciprocal, comprehensive, and permanent.[21] Since CAFTA-DR entered into force, U.S. merchandise trade with the countries of the northern triangle has increased by nearly 48%, from $18 billion in 2006 to $26.6 billion in 2014; U.S. exports to the region have grown by 64% and U.S. imports from the region have grown by 30%.[22] The stock of U.S. direct investment in the northern triangle countries grew from $1.9 billion in 2006 to $4.9 billion in 2013—an increase of 153%. These trends vary somewhat by country. Honduras, for example, has seen little change in U.S. direct investment.[23]

There continue to be strong cultural ties between the United States and Central America, and many continue to leave the region for the United States, both through authorized and unauthorized means. In 2013, the foreign-born populations from El Salvador (1,252,067), Guatemala (902,293), and Honduras (533,598) ranked as the 6th, 10th, and 16th largest groups, respectively, of all foreign born groups in the United States.[24] According to Department of Homeland Security (DHS) estimates, 55% of Salvadorans, 64% of Guatemalans, and 67% of Hondurans residing in the United States are in the country illegally.[25]

U.S. deportations to the northern triangle countries have increased significantly in recent years. Since FY2007, the number of Salvadorans removed has increased by 36%, the number of Guatemalans removed has increased by 110%, and the number of Hondurans removed has increased 37%. In FY2014, about 27,200 Salvadorans, 54,400 Guatemalans, and 40,700 Hondurans were removed from the United States.[26]

Some Central Americans, who may otherwise be deported, have been allowed to stay in the United States with Temporary Protected Status (TPS). The U.S. government has continuously provided TPS to eligible Hondurans since 1998, when Hurricane Mitch struck Honduras, and to eligible Salvadorans since 2001, when El Salvador experienced a series of earthquakes. An estimated 61,000 Hondurans and 204,000 Salvadorans currently benefit from TPS.[27] Other Central Americans are likely to be eligible to benefit from President Obama's November 2014 executive actions on immigration.[28]

## U.S. Response to Surge in Unaccompanied Minors

Over the past year, U.S. policy makers have devoted considerable attention to the surge of unaccompanied minors arriving at the U.S. border. While much of the initial response focused on immigration enforcement and other U.S. domestic policies, both the Obama Administration and Congress have taken some steps intended to address the foreign policy dimensions of the situation.

### *Obama Administration's Initial Response*

The Obama Administration has responded to the increase in unaccompanied children traveling to the United States from Central America in a number of ways. Since June 2014, it has worked with the Salvadoran, Guatemalan, Honduran, and Mexican governments to establish a common understanding and coordinate a response. This diplomatic outreach has included visits to the region by Vice President Joseph Biden, Secretary of State John Kerry, Secretary of Homeland Security Jeh Johnson, and other high-level Administration officials. Likewise, President Obama hosted President Salvador Sánchez Ceren of El Salvador, President Otto Pérez Molina of Guatemala, and President Juan Orlando Hernández of Honduras at the White House in July 2014, and Vice President Biden met with them during a conference at the Inter-American Development Bank (IDB) in November 2014.

In addition to coordinating with leaders in the region, Administration officials have engaged in extensive public diplomacy. The President and other officials have warned Central Americans about the dangers involved in traveling to the United States, and have sought to correct possible misperceptions about U.S. immigration policies. Over the summer, U.S. Customs and Border Protection (CBP) launched the "Dangers Awareness Campaign," which included media outreach in metropolitan areas of the United States that have high concentrations of Central American immigrants, as well as billboards and public service announcements in El Salvador, Guatemala, and Honduras. Nearly 6,400 radio and television announcements aired in the northern triangle during the campaign, which ran from June 30-October 12, 2014.[29] On January 5, 2015, the Department of Homeland Security (DHS) joined with the State Department to launch the "Executive Action on Immigration: Know the Facts" awareness campaign. Like the "Dangers Awareness Campaign," it includes print, radio, and television announcements designed to explain U.S. immigration policies and dispel potential misinformation.[30] Central American governments have bolstered U.S. efforts by running complementary public awareness campaigns.

In another attempt to dissuade Central American children from traveling to the United States illegally, the Administration established an in-country refugee/parole program in El Salvador, Guatemala, and Honduras. The program, which officially launched in December 2014, allows children who have a parent that is lawfully present in the United States to be considered for refugee status while still residing in their countries of origin. Children who are found to be ineligible for refugee status but are at risk of harm can be considered for parole. It is unclear how many Central American children will qualify for the program.[31]

The Obama Administration has also intensified its efforts to target and dismantle human smuggling operations. In July 2014, DHS and the Department of Justice (DOJ) launched "Operation Coyote," a joint campaign to surge resources toward the investigation, arrest, and prosecution of smuggling networks that facilitate the movement of unaccompanied children from Central America to the United States. As of December 2014, the operation had resulted in 977 criminal arrests and the seizure of over $1 million from 609 bank accounts.[32] The Administration has also pushed the governments of Mexico and the northern triangle nations to intensify their anti-smuggling efforts. Some security analysts maintain that anti-smuggling operations are unlikely to have a significant impact on migration flows in the long run. They assert that since smuggling will remain a high demand and lucrative business as long as people want to migrate, other organized criminal groups or illicit actors will step in to fill the void left by any dismantled networks.[33]

At the same time, the Administration has sought to increase U.S. assistance for Central America. During his trip to Guatemala in June 2014, Vice President Biden announced that the United States would provide $9.6 million of additional aid to Central American nations to strengthen programs for deported migrants.[34] Using this funding, which was reprogrammed from existing FY2014 appropriations, USAID signed a $7.6 million agreement with the International Organization for Migration (IOM). IOM will ensure that reception centers in El Salvador, Guatemala, and Honduras are capable of processing and providing immediate care, child protection services, and other assistance to returning families and children.[35]

In July 2014, the Administration submitted an emergency supplemental appropriations request to Congress that included $300 million to support economic prosperity, governance, security, and repatriation efforts in Central

America.[36] The Senate considered a bill, S. 2648, that would have provided $300 million for programs in Central America, but it was never adopted. The House bill, H.R. 5230, would not have provided any new assistance for programs in Central America but would have allowed $40 million of previously appropriated funding to be made available for repatriation and reintegration activities. It was adopted in August 2014 but never considered in the Senate.

### *FY2015 Appropriations Legislation*

Although Congress opted not to appropriate supplemental funding for programs in Central America in FY2014, it included additional resources for the region in its FY2015 appropriations measure. The Consolidated and Further Continuing Appropriations Act, 2015 (P.L. 113-235) appears to fully fund the Administration's request for minor increases in bilateral assistance for El Salvador, Guatemala, and Honduras. It also provides $130 million above the Administration's FY2015 request for CARSI (see *Table 1*) and $79 million above the request to, among other things, support Mexico's efforts to secure its southern border.

The legislation directs the Secretary of State to use the funds appropriated for the region to implement a strategy to "address the key factors in the countries in Central America contributing to the migration of unaccompanied, undocumented minors to the United States." The strategy, which is to be submitted to Congress by mid-March 2015, is required to include:

- a clear mission statement, achievable goals and objectives, benchmarks, timelines, and a spending plan;
- a path forward for addressing the need for greater border security for the countries in Central America and Mexico, particularly the southern borders of Mexico;
- economic and social development programs, with a focus on communities that have been major contributors of unaccompanied migrants and where there is significant gang activity;
- judicial and police reform and capacity building programs, with a focus on strengthening judicial independence and community policing;
- activities to combat human trafficking in Central America, including through the use of forensic technology; and

- actions to support the safe repatriation and reintegration of minors into families or family-like settings.

Within 60 days of submitting the strategy and every 120 days thereafter, the Secretary of State is required to report to Congress on the progress made toward achieving the objectives of the strategy. These reports are required to include the funding provided to each country and the steps taken by each government in the region to improve border security, reduce the flow of unauthorized migrants, conduct public awareness campaigns, and cooperate with U.S. agencies on the repatriation and reintegration of their citizens. The act also directs the Secretary of State to suspend assistance to any government that fails to carry out the required actions.

### *FY2016 Administration Request*

Asserting that the FY2014 surge in unaccompanied minors was a reminder that "the security and prosperity of Central America are inextricably linked to our own," the Administration has requested $1 billion in foreign assistance for the region in FY2016.[37] The funding would be used to implement a new "U.S. Strategy for Engagement in Central America," a whole-of-government approach designed to increase economic opportunity, reduce extreme violence, and strengthen the effectiveness of state institutions in Central America. The objectives of the strategy are consistent with the directives included in the FY2015 appropriations measure and the priorities established in the "Plan of the Alliance for Prosperity in the Northern Triangle" that was proposed by the governments of El Salvador, Guatemala, and Honduras in September 2014 (see "Central American Capacity to Address Root Causes"). The request includes:

- *$400 million for increasing economic opportunity.* These funds would support efforts to facilitate trade, promote customs and border integration, improve business environments, and integrate regional value chains and electricity markets. They would also support programs to reduce poverty, improve early grade literacy, and provide vocational training and other types of alternative education.
- *$300 million for improving security conditions.* These funds would support training for law enforcement personnel, border and maritime interdiction operations, and efforts to strengthen investigative and prosecutorial capacity. They would also support community policing, the development of municipal crime prevention committees, and the

expansion of outreach centers that provide opportunities for at-risk youth.

- *$250 million for strengthening governance.* These funds would support efforts to carry out significant civil service reforms, improve revenue collection and financial management, and strengthen rule-of-law institutions and government service delivery. They would also provide support to civil society groups designed to strengthen their capacities to hold governments accountable.
- It appears as though the remaining $50 million would be dedicated to ongoing health and military assistance programs.

While the U.S. government already supports many of these types of activities in Central America (see "Current Policy Framework"), the FY2016 request would allow existing programs to be scaled up significantly and would place greater emphasis on economic prosperity and governance while continuing to address security concerns. Compared to FY2014, bilateral aid for El Salvador would increase from $22 million to $119 million, bilateral aid for Guatemala would increase from $65 million to $221 million, and bilateral aid for Honduras would increase from $42 million to $163 million. Nearly all of the increased bilateral aid would be provided through the Development Assistance account, which is administered by USAID (see *Figure 4 and Table 2*).

About half of the Administration's $1 billion request for Central America would be provided through regional programs. Aid provided through CARSI, which has been the principal component of U.S. engagement with the region in recent years, would increase from $162 million in FY2014 to $286 million in FY2016. Aid provided through USAID's Central America Regional program would increase from $34 million to $65 million. The request also includes $127 million that would be provided through the State Department's Western Hemisphere Regional program to support prosperity and governance in Central America (see Figure 4 and Table 2). Although it is unclear how much funding from the regional programs would go to each country, the majority likely would be allocated to El Salvador, Guatemala, and Honduras.

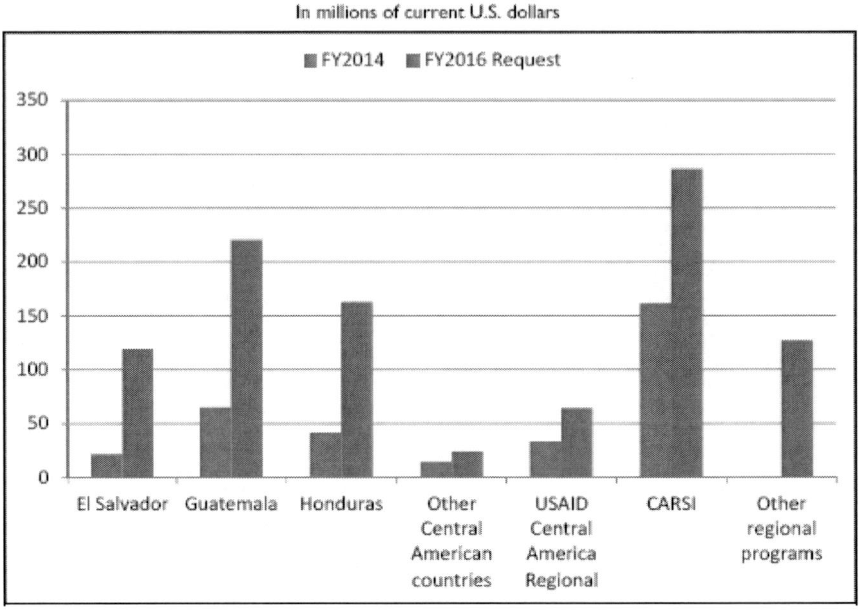


Source: CRS analysis of U.S. Department of State, Congressional Budget Justification: Department of State, Foreign Operations, and Related Programs, Fiscal Year 2016, February 2, 2015.

Notes: FY2014 figures are estimates.

Figure 4. U.S. Aid to Central America: FY2014 and FY2016 Request.

**Table 2. U.S. Assistance for Central America in the FY2016 Request In millions of current U.S. dollars**

| | *DA* | *GHP* | *ESF* | *INCLE* | *FMF* | *IMET* | *Total* |
|---|---|---|---|---|---|---|---|
| El Salvador | 116.5 | 0.0 | 0.0 | 0.0 | 1.9 | 0.8 | 119.2 |
| Guatemala | 205.1 | 13.0 | 0.0 | 0.0 | 1.7 | 0.8 | 220.6 |
| Honduras | 157.7 | 0.0 | 0.0 | 0.0 | 4.5 | 0.8 | 163.0 |
| Other countries[a] | 18.2 | 0.0 | 0.0 | 0.0 | 4.5 | 1.4 | 24.1 |
| USAID Central | 43.5 | 21.0 | 0.0 | 0.0 | 0.0 | 0.0 | 64.5 |
| America Regional | | | | | | | |
| State Western | 0.0 | 0.0 | 208.6 | 205.0 | 0.0 | 0.0 | 413.6 |
| Hemisphere | | | | | | | |
| Regionalb | | | | | | | |
| [CARSI] | [0.0] | [0.0] | [81.5] | [205.0] | [0.0] | [0.0] | [286.5] |
| [Other] | [0.0] | [0.0] | [127.1] | [0.0] | [0.0] | [0.0] | [127.1] |
| Total | 541.0 | 34.0 | 208.6 | 205.0 | 12.6 | 3.7 | 1,004.9 |

Source: U.S. Department of State, Congressional Budget Justification: Department of State, Foreign Operations, and Related Programs, Fiscal Year 2016, February 2, 2015.

Notes: These figures could change as more information about the request is released. DA=Development Assistance; GHP=Global Health Programs; ESF=Economic Support Fund; INCLE=International Narcotics Control and Law Enforcement; FMF=Foreign Military Financing; and IMET=International Military Education and Training.

[a] Includes assistance for Belize, Costa Rica, Nicaragua, and Panama.

[b] The State Department's Western Hemisphere Regional program includes funding for a variety of initiatives in the Western Hemisphere. These figures only include the portions of the program dedicated to CARSI and other assistance efforts in Central America.

# POLICY CONSIDERATIONS

As Congress debates the Administration's FY2016 request and other legislative options to address the foreign policy dimensions of the surge in unaccompanied minors, there are a variety of interrelated issues that it might take into consideration. These include the capacity of Central American nations to receive and reintegrate unaccompanied children deported from the United States, the capacity of Central American nations to address the root causes of the exodus, the role of Mexico as a transit country, and selected ongoing international humanitarian efforts.

## Central American Capacity to Receive and Reintegrate Deportees

Administration officials maintain that the majority of unaccompanied minors apprehended in the United States will be returned to their home countries,[38] raising the question of how well-equipped El Salvador, Guatemala, and Honduras are to meet the needs of the individuals sent back. Many humanitarian experts warn that "rapid deportation could threaten the wellbeing of returnee children" unless recipient countries are capable of providing adequate support.[39] A major challenge is to increase the response capacity of these countries to protect, assist, and provide solutions for displaced persons, including children, in a variety of contexts, primarily those that are being returned from another country (most often Mexico, and to a lesser extent, the United States), internally displaced persons (IDPs), those at risk of displacement, and those entering the asylum channel because they are fleeing a situation elsewhere.[40]

In FY2013, the most recent year for which U.S. government data are available by country, DHS deported 159 unaccompanied children to El Salvador, 661 to Guatemala, and 461 to Honduras, for a total of 1,281.[41] According to the State Department's Unaccompanied Alien Children Monitoring Group, U.S. deportations of unaccompanied minors decreased in FY2014, to a total of 510 for all three countries.[42] Those deported were apprehended prior to the FY2014 surge and were returned in small numbers. Despite the limited number of unaccompanied children deported thus far, all three countries have reported that their resources are strained trying to keep up with the demand for services resulting from overall increases in deportations. Moreover, the U.S., Salvadoran, Guatemalan, and Honduran governments are concerned that as the cases of the nearly 52,000 Central American children apprehended in FY2014 are processed, minors will be deported in numbers larger than the receiving countries are equipped to handle.

The U.S. government has previously indicated that El Salvador and Honduras are not capable of handling large influxes of deportations, stating in its extensions of TPS that each of those countries "remains unable, temporarily, to handle the return of its nationals."[43] Observers have expressed particular concern about whether the northern triangle countries are capable of protecting those most at risk. According to the U.N. High Commissioner for Refugees (UNHCR), "neither national nor local authorities have, at this point, the capacity to reintegrate children in a safe manner in any [northern triangle] country."[44]

Recognizing this lack of capacity, the three northern triangle governments have begun developing plans to better assist deported children and asking international donors and institutions for support in carrying them out. As previously mentioned, USAID has initiated programs in all three countries to improve their capacities to receive unaccompanied minors. U.S. assistance, largely provided through the International Organization for Migration (IOM), is providing training and equipment and supporting the development of infrastructure.

To date, the Guatemalan government appears to be providing more comprehensive services to its returned citizens than its two neighbors. Some of these services were initiated in 2011 by the IOM with funding from USAID, but the Guatemalan government assumed responsibility for them after that program ended in July 2013. At a reception center at a Guatemalan Air Force base in Guatemala City, numerous government agencies provide or facilitate services including motivational welcome talks, refreshments, free phone calls, on-site banking for changing money, and psychological care. Immigration officials help process returnees; National Registry officials begin the process of getting returnees a national identification card; the Foreign Affairs Ministry explains available services and offers help, such as buying transportation tickets to remote areas; and the Health Ministry has a clinical office on the premises. The National Council for Attention to Migrants provides some long-term support, dedicating about 20% of its budget to reintegration services for repatriates. Unaccompanied minors are processed in an area separate from adults, and the Guatemalan Attorney General's office takes custody of children until a family member or other guardian can be found. Services for such children are severely limited, however, as there is a single shelter that holds just 20-30 children and allows them to stay up to two days.[45]

According to USAID, IOM is working with the Guatemalan government again, distributing hygiene kits, phone cards, and transportation assistance to deported people. It is expanding its services to the shelter in Quetzaltenango where most unaccompanied children from Mexico arrive by land. IOM will train staff in the Guatemalan government child protection services. World Vision will begin building a reception site at the Air Force base for returning women and children.

Honduras currently has four reception centers for individuals removed from Mexico and the United States.[46] Upon their arrival, the deportees undergo medical, psychological, and social assessments. Labor Ministry officials collect information about the adults to assist them in obtaining employment, and Education Ministry officials collect information about minors to assist them in returning to school. The Honduran President has promised to enroll individuals that qualify in the country's various social welfare programs. Deportees may stay in temporary shelters for up to two days. Upon their departure, they are provided a small transportation stipend to return to their communities of origin, and—in certain cases—bags of food. The newly created National Directorate for Children, Adolescents, and Family (DINAF) is responsible for receiving unaccompanied children and placing them with their families or in care centers (if no family can be located).[47]

According to UNHCR, the shelter in San Pedro Sula where unaccompanied children from Mexico and the United States are currently sent has very limited services; UNHCR and other organizations are working to improve conditions at that shelter.[48] Since last year, IOM has been assessing various ports of entry for deported people and will commence construction on improvements soon. IOM has been delivering hygiene kits to the San Pedro Sula shelter and will soon provide appliances there.

The Salvadoran government's services for deported people are rudimentary. Upon arrival, they receive a meal, emergency medical attention, and information from the Department of Migration about the services it offers. Reintegration assistance includes psychological services and referrals to education and job training programs. El Salvador's program for deportees does not appear to provide specialized services for unaccompanied minors. According to USAID, data collected from IOM indicates that over 90% of unaccompanied minors don't need long-term shelter and are reunited with family within 12 to 24 hours.[49] Children who cannot be reunited with family members are placed in two shelters/orphanages run by the national child protection agency. Some Salvadoran municipalities have formed Committees on Children's Rights, and the government has set up networks between government and civil society actors to help deported minors in those locales.[50] According to USAID, however, these networks have insufficient resources to thoroughly track and support them.

IOM is currently renovating one of the child protection agency's facilities and will soon begin rehabilitation of a reception site for unaccompanied children in San Salvador.

Given the limited capacities of the region's governments, some non-governmental organizations (NGOs) have stepped in to offer support to unaccompanied minors. In Honduras, for example, Casa Alianza has been providing follow-up services to a small number of children reunited with their families in San Pedro Sula. In Guatemala, Global Fund for Children (GFC) and Kids in Need of Defense (KIND) work with four nonprofit community-based organizations to provide services through the Guatemalan Child Return and Reintegration Project. Services include pro bono legal help during the removal process in the United States, and upon return to Guatemala, temporary shelter, family reunification assistance, psychological services, education, job training, employment assistance, and workshops to support social reintegration. GFC and KIND say they will take the best practices learned from the pilot project and promote similar projects elsewhere in the region.[51]

## Central American Capacity to Address Root Causes

While addressing short-term issues, such as how to absorb a large influx of deportees, will be challenging, addressing the root causes pushing unaccompanied children to leave El Salvador, Guatemala, and Honduras will likely be even more difficult. All three countries are characterized by poor security and socioeconomic conditions, with high violent crime rates, significant transnational gang activity, low economic growth rates, and high levels of poverty and inequality.[52] These conditions are interrelated, as high levels of inequality are strongly correlated with high levels of violence,[53] and insecurity has discouraged foreign investment and inhibited development.[54] Many analysts assert that the northern triangle governments lack the institutions, resources, and political will necessary to tackle these deep-seated problems.[55] Nevertheless, as discussed below, the Salvadoran, Guatemalan, and Honduran governments have worked together to develop the "Plan of the Alliance for Prosperity in the Northern Triangle," which would combine government and private sector efforts with donor-funded initiatives to address longstanding development challenges.

In recent years, much has been written about the governance problems that have made the northern triangle countries susceptible to the influence of drug traffickers and other criminal elements and unable to guarantee citizen security—a basic function of any government.[56] Many analysts note that the governments of these countries do not have operational control over their borders and territories. This lack of territorial control is partially a result of police and military forces being generally undermanned and/or ill-equipped to establish an effective presence in remote regions or to challenge well-armed criminal groups. Some of these criminal organizations have laundered money through U.S. banks and obtained illegal U.S. firearms.[57]

Resource constraints aside, there have also been serious concerns about corruption in the security forces, justice sector institutions, and political systems in Central America.[58] Impunity in the criminal justice systems in the northern triangle countries has generally been very high (95% or more); however, Guatemala has reduced impunity rates in recent years.[59] This corruption and impunity has occurred partially as a result of incomplete institutional reforms implemented after armed conflicts ended in El Salvador and Guatemala in the 1990s. Criminal groups' efforts to influence public officials and elections, particularly at the local level, have also contributed to corruption.

Even if the northern triangle countries had stronger criminal justice systems capable of addressing insecurity, some analysts have argued that governments in those countries might not be willing to make the efforts necessary to address poverty and inequality—two other factors "pushing" individuals to leave.[60] Central American political elites have long benefitted from emigration to the United States, which serves as a "safety valve" that reduces social pressure to address high rates of unemployment and job losses and devastation wrought by periodic natural disasters. It also provides supplementary income to families in the form of remittances sent by workers in the United States. In 2013, remittances were equivalent to about 16% of gross domestic product (GDP) in El Salvador, 9% of GDP in Guatemala, and 17% of GDP in Honduras.[61]

Moreover, the governments of the northern triangle countries generally have been unable or unwilling to increase revenues, which are currently inadequate to meet public needs. Elites in all three countries have vigorously opposed efforts to raise taxes even though tax rates in the northern triangle countries are comparatively low and regressive.[62] These elites tend to rely on private service providers for everything from education to security, thereby making them reluctant to invest in public institutions. This has left the northern triangle societies locked in a vicious circle in which governments underperform, citizen confidence in government institutions erodes, those with resources refuse to invest in public institutions, and governance and socioeconomic and security conditions continue to deteriorate.

Despite these limitations, governments in the northern triangle have made some efforts to improve conditions in their countries. In El Salvador, the government is prioritizing community policing and implementing public-private partnerships to fund infrastructure and other projects, particularly in the southern coastal regions that will benefit from the second MCC compact signed in September 2014.[63] The Honduran government has increased taxes and pledged to devote a third of the funds collected from a security tax, enacted and then partially repealed in 2011, to support crime and violence prevention programs.[64] The Guatemalan government has made some progress in addressing crime and impunity with the help of the U.N.-supported International Commission Against Impunity in Guatemala (CICIG), though some fear that progress could be rolled back now that Claudia Paz y Paz—who worked closely with CICIG on a number of high profile cases—is no longer Attorney General.[65]

Most recently, the Salvadoran, Guatemalan, and Honduran governments, with substantial technical assistance from the Inter-American Development Bank (IDB), worked together to produce the "Plan of the Alliance for

Prosperity in the Northern Triangle" in September 2014. The four goals of the plan are to (1) stimulate the productive sector, (2) develop opportunities for the people of Central America, (3) improve public safety and access to the justice system, and (4) strengthen institutions to increase people's trust in the state. The plan also outlines actions for achieving those goals. Among other ideas, they include reducing energy costs, modernizing infrastructure, increasing technical and vocational training, providing incentives to keep kids in school, strengthening violence prevention plans and public safety institutions, overhauling tax systems, and increasing government transparency. Although some of these efforts are reportedly already underway, the countries maintain that they will need significant additional resources from allied countries, multilateral organizations, and other development partners.[66] The Guatemalan government has reportedly stated that each of the three northern triangle countries will need about $5 billion over four years to implement the plan.[67]

## Role of Mexico as a Transit Country

Historically, Mexico's dual status as the largest source of U.S. migrants and a continental neighbor has meant that U.S. immigration policy—including stepped up border and interior enforcement—has primarily affected Mexicans.[68] In recent years, however, emigration from Mexico has declined dramatically.[69] As a result, many U.S. policy makers have increasingly viewed Mexico as a partner that has an important role to play in securing its southern border and combating Central American transmigration through its territory. The Mexican government collaborates with U.S. law enforcement agencies to combat alien smuggling, human trafficking, and illegal migration by third country nationals, particularly from Central America. During a presidential visit in early January 2015, President Obama praised Mexico's efforts to secure its southern border and help combat illegal transmigration through its territory.[70]

The Mexican government appears to be attempting to balance enforcement and humanitarian concerns in its migration policies. In addition to passing new laws to stiffen penalties for alien smuggling (2010) and human trafficking (2012), Mexico enacted a comprehensive migration reform in 2011. Contrary to some media reports, the reform did not create a transit visa for migrants crossing through Mexico—as some civil society groups had been advocating. Mexico still requires visas for Central Americans entering its territory who do not possess a valid U.S. visa. Exceptions include those from Guatemala or Belize who possess temporary work permits, or those with regional visitor's cards allowing them to visit Mexico's border region for up to 72 hours.

According to many experts, Mexico's migration policies have produced mixed results, with their effectiveness hindered by corruption among migration officials and police.[71] The Mexican government has purged some corrupt staff from the National Migration Institute (INM) in the Interior Ministry over the past year, but its failure to more fully overhaul the agency has slowed implementation of the 2011 reform.[72] Mexico has recently stepped up immigration enforcement along highways and train routes used by some Central American migrants. From January through May 2014, the Mexican government arrested 431 people for breaking provisions in the migration law; most of those individuals were accused of smuggling-related crimes.[73] Even when arrests are made, however, the weakness of Mexico's criminal justice system has resulted in extremely low conviction rates.[74]

**Alien Smuggling and Trafficking in Persons**

Alien smuggling is often confused with trafficking in persons. Alien smuggling involves the provision of a service, generally transportation, to people who knowingly consent to that service in order to gain illegal entry into a foreign country. It ends with the arrival of the foreign national at his or her destination. Smugglers get clients through word of mouth, social networks, and even the Internet; often they are sought out by parents wanting to reunite with their children.[75] Trafficking in persons is a crime committed against victims who are exploited. It does not have to involve movement from one country to another; however, when it does, a victim is often lured or made to travel through the use of "force, fraud, or coercion."[76] Under U.S. immigration law, a trafficked migrant is a victim while an alien who consents to being smuggled is complicit in a criminal activity and may therefore be subject to prosecution and deportation. Distinguishing the difference between a trafficking victim and a smuggled migrant can be difficult, particularly in cases involving unaccompanied children. The State Department's June 2014 Trafficking in Persons Report highlighted migrants from Central America as highly vulnerable to human trafficking in Mexico.

As U.S. border security has tightened, unauthorized migrants have become increasingly dependent upon smugglers (coyotes) to lead them through Mexico to the United States.[77] U.S. officials estimate that 75-80% of unaccompanied minors now travel with smugglers.[78] This increased demand has made alien smuggling more lucrative. Organized criminal groups, like Los Zetas, have sought to profit from the smuggling business, demanding payments from those passing through their territory and engaging in abduction and extortion.79 Some smugglers have sold migrants into situations of forced labor or prostitution (forms of human trafficking) to recover their costs; other smugglers' failure to pay Los Zetas has reportedly resulted in massacres of migrants.[80]

Although organized crime-related homicides in Mexico have declined at a national level since 2011, they have increased in Tamaulipas, a state traversed by many U.S.- bound Central Americans.

Experts also maintain that Mexico lacks the funding and institutions to address traditional migration flows, much less the increasing numbers of unaccompanied children that its agents are detaining. According to INM, Mexico removed 86,949 individuals from the northern triangle countries from January-November 2014, a 17.9% increase from the 73,695 removed from those countries during the same period of 2013.[81]

Mexico has temporary shelters dedicated to serving migrant children, but no foster care system in which to place those who might be granted asylum. Requests for asylum filed by youth from northern triangle countries in Mexico increased from 124 in 2008 to 883 in 2013 according to the UNHCR; 139 youth from those countries received asylum in 2013.[82] The Interior Ministry reported only 12 asylum requests in 2014, however.[83] Child protection officers from INM accompanied nearly 8,600 children to their countries of origin in 2013. From January-November 2014, INM detained more than 21,500 minors: 98% of whom originated in the northern triangle. Mexico returned more than 16,600 of those minors to their countries of origin.[84]

With U.S. support, the Mexican government has been implementing a southern border security plan since 2013 that has involved the establishment of 12 naval bases on the country's rivers and three security cordons that stretch more than 100 miles north of the Mexico-Guatemala and Mexico-Belize borders.[85] Total State Department support for mobile Non-Intrusive Inspection Equipment and related equipment and training for Mexico's southern border strategy was expected to exceed $86.6 million prior to the enactment of the FY2015 appropriations measure. As previously noted, Congress provided $79 million in that act (P.L. 113-235) above the Administration's FY2015 request for the Mérida Initiative in Mexico, including support for efforts to secure

Mexico's southern border. The U.S. Department of Defense (DOD) has also provided training to troops patrolling the border, communications equipment, and support for the development of Mexico's air mobility and surveillance capabilities.

## Selected International Humanitarian Efforts

The sharp increase in the number of unaccompanied children arriving at the U.S.-Mexico border in mid-2014 prompted the U.N. High Commissioner for Refugees (UNHCR) to call for a "robust regional humanitarian response" based on principles of protection. According to UNHCR, not every person crossing the U.S. border qualifies as a refugee, but the lines of distinction between and among refugees, asylum seekers, and migrants—particularly in the current situation—are not always clear. UNHCR has called for children and families who fear harm in their home countries to have access to an appropriate asylum system in the United States and other countries in the region. It has offered to support the United States and other asylum countries to help with immediate and longer term responses to this challenge.

The U.S. government and the governments of Honduras, Guatemala, El Salvador, and Mexico have each expressed concern for the protection of the human rights of these vulnerable children in their country of origin, during transit, and upon arrival in the destination country. During all phases of the journey, including while in detention and during the returns process, unaccompanied children require comprehensive assistance with food, medical care, shelter, protection, safety, legal assistance, and education. From a humanitarian perspective, this means addressing the humanitarian needs of the children and families while protecting their rights and dignity.

The situation of unaccompanied children is somewhat unique in the humanitarian context in that factors such as poverty, violence, and criminal activity create forced displacement rather than the impact of a natural disaster or conflict. Known as "other situations of violence," the conditions in the northern triangle and Mexico present what some experts regard as new causes for displacement that expand protection needs. The international humanitarian response includes U.N. agencies, such as UNHCR and the U.N. Children's Fund (UNICEF), and Humanitarian Country Teams of the northern triangle countries, which are working with national authorities to address the situation. International and local NGOs are also providing support and assistance in specific countries and on regional initiatives. A U.N. interagency working group is reportedly mapping the humanitarian actors involved.[86]

The operational priorities of different humanitarian organizations include, for example, the International Committee of the Red Cross (ICRC), which focuses on the protection and assistance of communities and individuals most vulnerable to and affected by armed violence and includes assistance to migrants, missing persons, and their families in the region. The International Organization for Migration (IOM), which often partners with UNHCR, is an intergovernmental organization that focuses on migration and related issues. As noted previously, IOM has led a number of projects in the region to address migration and displacement problems. The International Rescue Committee, Catholic Relief Services, Kids in Need of Defense (KIND) and World Vision are some of the international NGOs providing a range of assistance and support.

A number of regional and international entities are seeking to address the needs of unaccompanied children. UNHCR, for example, has called for cooperation with relevant governments; international partners, including international organizations and NGOs; and regional and national actors. Coordination within the U.N. system involves UNHCR under the Regional Protection Working Group and the U.N. Office for the Coordination of Humanitarian Assistance (UNOCHA) or other U.N. agencies taking the lead in specific countries. The Central American Integration System (SICA) may take the lead on regional policy discussions about displacement. The Organization of American States (OAS) has expressed concern through its affiliated Inter-American Commission on Human Rights (IACHR) and a Permanent Council resolution. Regional offices from the U.N. Development Group for Latin America and the Caribbean Group (UNDG LAC) are considering possible ways to link projects to the humanitarian situation. Meanwhile, a regional arm of the National Refugee Commissions will focus on improving systems available in each country for asylum seekers.[87]

International and regional organizations and groups are conducting meetings and activities to develop protection strategies for children who are or may be deported and may potentially face harm if sent home. These include the development of a possible regional initiative that could assist with identifying alternatives to detention, improving reception conditions, strengthening protection mechanisms at the national level, and monitoring the situation of deported children. UNHCR has emphasized that a regional approach should also focus on prevention strategies to address the root causes of the movement of children and families.

In December 2014, the governments of 28 countries and three territories of Latin America and the Caribbean met in Brasilia on the 30th anniversary of the 1984 Cartagena Declaration on Refugees and adopted by acclamation the Brazil Declaration and Plan of Action. Building on a consultative process in 2014 under the leadership of UNHCR and the Norwegian Refugee Council (NRC), the governments agreed to work together to "uphold the highest international and regional protection standards, implement innovative solutions for refugees and displaced persons, and end the plight of stateless persons in the region." The Plan of Action retains the expanded definition of "refugee" of the Cartagena Declaration, which goes beyond the 1951 U.N. Convention Relating to the Status of Refugees and the 1967 Protocol, and incorporates a new framework for regional action in the protection of vulnerable groups and individuals.[88]

## OUTLOOK

U.S. policy makers continue to face difficult decisions about how to respond to the sharp increase of unaccompanied children traveling to the United States. Nearly 69,000 such children were apprehended last fiscal year, with 75% of them coming from Central America. The Obama Administration's initial response, which included public awareness campaigns and anti-smuggling operations, appears to have reduced the number of children making the journey, at least temporarily. Nevertheless, many analysts think the United States is likely to receive significant mixed migration flows of refugees, asylum seekers, and migrants in the future unless there are substantial improvements in citizen security and socioeconomic opportunities for the large youth populations in the northern triangle countries.

Strengthening Central American nations' capacities to receive and reintegrate deportees is likely to be a major focus of the short-term U.S. policy response. The Administration has reprogrammed some assistance to assist partner countries with such efforts, and the FY2015 appropriations measure appears to provide additional support. Likewise, various international organizations are offering assistance to northern triangle governments as they expand their support services for repatriated citizens. Nevertheless, reports that some children face persecution and even death upon their return to Central America raise questions as to whether the countries will be able to quickly ramp up their capacities to provide adequate attention and protection to deportees.[89]

Improving socioeconomic and security conditions in Central America will be a long-term and difficult endeavor. Given that the United States has historically played an influential role in Central America and that U.S. drug demand has contributed to regional security challenges, Central American leaders and others contend that the United States should assume some of the responsibility for addressing the situation.[90] The Administration argues that assisting the region is also in the U.S. interest, since instability in Central America is likely to affect the United States.

Current U.S. policy provides support for Central American efforts to improve governance, economic opportunity, and citizen security through several assistance programs. Administration officials assert that "these programs are having an impact on some of the systemic conditions ... [but] they've been limited in scope because of the amount of funding available for them."[91] Accordingly, the Administration has requested $1 billion for the region in FY2016. Congress called for a comprehensive strategy to address conditions in Central America in its FY2015 appropriations measure, but it is far from certain whether it will approve the Administration's FY2016 request given current fiscal constraints and competing budget priorities.

While many analysts argue that Central American nations will require external support to address their challenges, they also maintain that significant improvements in security and socioeconomic conditions ultimately will depend on Central American leaders carrying out substantial internal reforms. Government leaders, civil society organizations, and business elites in Central America will need to develop concrete policies to raise revenues, reduce corruption, strengthen institutions, and expand educational and economic opportunities. Central American leaders have committed to such reforms as part of their proposed "Plan of the Alliance for Prosperity in the Northern Triangle." If they fail to follow through on those commitments, however, U.S. initiatives in the region may fail to produce policy makers' desired results.[92]

## End Notes

1 In this report, "unaccompanied children" and "unaccompanied minors" are used interchangeably to refer to foreign nationals under the age of 18 who are with neither a parent nor a legal guardian at the time they are apprehended. Other CRS reports may refer to the same group of minors as unaccompanied alien children (UAC).

2 CRS Report IN10107, Unaccompanied Alien Children: A Processing Flow Chart, by Lisa Seghetti.

[3] Jens Manuel Krogstad, Ana Gonzalez-Barrera, and Mark Hugo Lopez, Children 12 and Under are Fastest Growing Group of Unaccompanied Minors at U.S. Border, Pew Research Center, July 22, 2014; and At the Border, a Sharp Rise in Unaccompanied Girls Fleeing Honduras, Pew Research Center, July 25, 2014.

[4] U.S. Conference of Catholic Bishops, Mission to Central America: The Flight of Unaccompanied Children to the United States, Report of the Committee on Migration, November 2013; United Nations High Commissioner for Refugees (UNHCR), Children on the Run: Unaccompanied Children Leaving Central America and Mexico and the Need for International Protection, March 12, 2014; and Dinorah Azpuru, "Beyond the Blame Game: Visualizing the Complexity of the Border Crisis," Americas Quarterly, August 6, 2014. For more information, see CRS Report R43628, Unaccompanied Alien Children: Potential Factors Contributing to Recent Immigration, coordinated by William A. Kandel.

[5] U.S. Customs and Border Protection, "Southwest Border Unaccompanied Alien Children," press release, February 2015.

[6] See, for example, Dennis Stinchcomb and Eric Hershberg, Unaccompanied Migrant Children from Central America: Context, Causes, and Responses, American University, Center for Latin American and Latino Studies, CLALS Working Paper Series No. 7, November 2014.

[7] For information on the U.S. domestic policy response, see CRS Report R43599, Unaccompanied Alien Children: An Overview, by Lisa Seghetti, Alison Siskin, and Ruth Ellen Wasem.

[8] U.S. Agency for International Development (USAID), U.S. Overseas Loans and Grants: Obligations and Loan Authorizations, July 1, 1945-September 30, 2012, http://gbk.eads.usaidallnet.gov/.

[9] Priscilla B. Hayner, Unspeakable Truths: Facing the Challenge of Truth Commissions (New York: Routledge, 2002).

[10] Susan Gzesh, "Central Americans and Asylum Policy in the Reagan Era," Migration Information Source, April 1, 2006.

[11] U.N. Office on Drugs and Crime (UNODC), Crime and Development in Central America: Caught in the Crossfire, May 2007, p.40.

[12] Ana Arana, "How the Street Gangs Took Central America," Foreign Affairs, vol. 84, no. 3 (May/June 2005); Tim Johnson, "U.S. Export: Central America's Gang Problem Began in Los Angeles," McClatchy, August 5, 2014.

[13] U.S. Department of State, Arturo Valenzuela, Assistant Secretary of State, Bureau of Western Hemisphere Affairs, "U.S.-Latin American Relations: A Look Ahead," January 6, 2011.

[14] The Partnership for Growth is an Obama Administration initiative that seeks to foster sustained economic growth and development in top-performing low-income countries. It involves greater collaboration but does not necessarily include increased U.S. assistance. For more information, see CRS Report R43616, El Salvador: Background and U.S. Relations, by Clare Ribando Seelke.

[15] For more information on CARSI, see CRS Report R41731, Central America Regional Security Initiative: Background and Policy Issues for Congress, by Peter J. Meyer and Clare Ribando Seelke.

[16] U.S. Department of State, Congressional Budget Justification for Foreign Operations, Appendix 3: Regional Perspectives, Fiscal Year 2015, April 2014.

[17] For more information on the MCC, see CRS Report RL32427, Millennium Challenge Corporation, by Curt Tarnoff.

[18] The compact was originally for \$215 million but was reduced to \$205 million when the final \$10 million was terminated following the 2009 coup in Honduras.

[19] MCC, "El Salvador Investment Compact," https://www.mcc.gov/pages/countries/program/el-salvador-investmentcompact.

[20] MCC, "Countries and Country Tools," http://www.mcc.gov/pages/countries, and "Readout of the MCC Board of Directors December Quarterly Meeting," December 11, 2014.

[21] For more information on CAFTA-DR, see CRS Report R42468, The Dominican Republic-Central America-United States Free Trade Agreement (CAFTA DR): Developments in Trade and Investment.

[22] U.S. Department of Commerce data, as presented by Global Trade Atlas, February 2015.

[23] U.S. Bureau of Economic Analysis, "Balance of Payments and Direct Investment Position Data," February 2015.

[24] U.S. Census Bureau, "Place of Birth for the Foreign-Born Population in the United States," 2013 American Community Survey 1-Year Estimates, 2014.

[25] Bryan Baker and Nancy Rytina, Estimates of the Unauthorized Immigrant Population Residing in the United States: January 2012, Department of Homeland Security (DHS), Office of Immigration Statistics, March 2013.

[26] CRS calculations based on FY2011 removal data from DHS, Office of Immigration Statistics and FY2014 removal data from DHS, Immigration and Customs Enforcement (ICE).

[27] CRS Report RS20844, Temporary Protected Status: Current Immigration Policy and Issues, by Lisa Seghetti, Karma Ester, and Ruth Ellen Wasem.

[28] For more information on the President's executive action, see CRS Report R43852, The President's Immigration Accountability Executive Action of November 20, 2014: Overview and Issues, coordinated by William A. Kandel.

[29] CBP, "CBP Commissioner Discusses Dangers of Crossing U.S. Border, Awareness Campaign," July 2, 2014; CRS correspondence with CBP official, November 2014.

[30] DHS, "Departments of State, Homeland Security Launch Executive Action on Immigration: Know the Facts Awareness Campaign," press release, January 5, 2015.

[31] U.S. Department of State, Bureau of Population, Refugees, and Migration, "In-Country Refugee/Parole Program for Minors in El Salvador, Guatemala, and Honduras with Parents Lawfully Present in the United States," fact sheet, November 14, 2014. For more information on refugee admissions, see CRS Report RL31269, Refugee Admissions and Resettlement Policy, by Andorra Bruno.

[32] DHS, "Statement by Secretary Johnson Regarding Today's Trip to Texas," December 15, 2014.

[33] Kyra Gurney, "US 'Operation Coyote' Fails to Address Child Migrant Crisis," Insight Crime, July 23, 2014.

[34] White House, Office of the Press Secretary, "Fact Sheet: Unaccompanied Children from Central America," June 20, 2014.

[35] USAID, "Regional Program Narrative: USAID Central America Regional," CN #29, November 20, 2014.

[36] U.S. Department of State, Supplemental Request Justification for Department of State, Foreign Operations, and Related Programs, Fiscal Year 2014, July 8, 2014.

[37] Joseph R. Biden Jr., "Joe Biden: A Plan for Central America," New York Times, January 29, 2015.

[38] "Senior State Department Official Holds a Background Briefing en Route to Panama – News Briefing," CQ Transcriptions, June 30, 2014.

[39] U.N. Office for the Coordination of Humanitarian Affairs (OCHA), Central America and Mexico Unaccompanied Child Migration, Situation Report No. 01, July 29, 2014.

[40] In crises resulting from conflict or natural disasters, population movements often occur within the affected country or flow to countries in close proximity. IDPs, who are often forced to move because of internal violence, seek safety within their state's borders.

[41] Data provided to CRS by Immigration and Customs Enforcement (ICE) Legislative Affairs, October 20, 2014.

[42] CRS communication with State Department Unaccompanied Alien Children Monitoring Group official, February 4, 2015.

[43] DHS, "Extension of the Designation of El Salvador for Temporary Protected Status," Federal Register vol. 78, no. 104, May 30, 2013, doc. no. 2013-12793; and "Extension of the Designation of Honduras for Temporary Protected Status," Federal Register vol. 78, no. 64, April 3, 2013, doc. no.2013-07673.

[44] CRS communication with UNHCR official, February 4, 2015.

[45] International Organization for Migration (IOM), "Press Conference on the Guatemalan Repatriates Project," June 3, 2011; Lee Hopkins, "Making Guatemala 'Home' Again: Service Approaches for Sustainable Reintegration of Repatriates in Guatemala," Columbia University Partnership for International Development Online Journal, February 9, 2014, p. 2.

[46] CRS communication with Honduran official, July 30, 2014.

[47] Gobierno de la República de Honduras, Presidencia de la República, "Gobierno de Honduras está Preparado para Recibir a Compatriotas Deportados de Estados Unidos," July 4, 2014; Augustin Lagos N., "Minucioso Protocolo Aplican a Migrantes," El Heraldo, July 16, 2014; "Honduras Define Nueva Estrategia de Atención a Niñez para Disuadir Migración," Agence France Presse, July 22, 2014.

[48] CRS communication with UNHCR official, February 4, 2015.

[49] CRS communication with USAID/El Salvador official, Feb. 4, 2015.

[50] HHS, January 2013, op. cit.

[51] Kids in Need of Defense, "Guatemalan Child Return and Reintegration Project," http://www.supportkind.org/en/ kind-in-action/guatemala-return-and-reintegration-project.

[52] For more information, see CRS Report R43628, Unaccompanied Alien Children: Potential Factors Contributing to Recent Immigration, coordinated by William A. Kandel.

[53] UNODC, Global Study on Homicide: Trends, Contexts, Data, 2011, p. 30.

[54] U.N. Economic Commission on Latin America and the Caribbean (ECLAC), 2013 Foreign Direct Investment in Latin America and the Caribbean, May 2014; U.S. Department of State, Partnership for Growth: El Salvador Constraints Analysis, July 2011.

[55] José Miguel Cruz, "The Real Failure in Central America," Miami Herald, July 24, 2014; Steven Dudley, "Guatemala, Honduras Presidents Blame US, Ignore Own Problems," Insight Crime, August 25, 2014.

[56] For more information, see CRS Report R41731, Central America Regional Security Initiative: Background and Policy Issues for Congress, by Peter J. Meyer and Clare Ribando Seelke.

[57] Brian Bennett, "Border Crisis: U.S. Targets Money Launderers to Track Child Smugglers," Los Angeles Times, July 22, 2014; "Gunrunning from the US to Central America," Latin News Daily Report, July 30, 2014.

[58] For recent examples of corruption, see country entries in U.S. Department of State, Bureau of International Narcotics and Law Enforcement Affairs, 2014 International Narcotics Control Strategy Report (INCSR), March 2014.

[59] Eric Olson et al., Crime and Violence in Central America's Northern Triangle, Woodrow Wilson Center Latin America Program, Woodrow Wilson Center Reports on the Americas #34, December 2014, p. 2.

[60] Joaquín Villalobos, "Niños Inocentes y Oligarcas Voraces," El País, July 12, 2014.

[61] CRS calculations based on remittance data from René Maldonado and Maria Luisa, Remittances to Latin America and the Caribbean in 2013: Still Below Pre-Crisis Levels, Inter-American Development Bank (IDB), Multilateral Investment Fund, 2014; and GDP data from International Monetary Fund (IMF), World Economic Outlook Database, April 2014, April 8, 2014.

[62] A recent study forecast tax revenues as a percentage of income for 2014 to be 15.1% for El Salvador (down from 15.8%), 10.9% for Guatemala (down slightly from 11.0%), and 15.9% for Honduras (up from 14.7%). Instituto Centroamericano de Estudios Fiscales (ICEFI), Centroamérica: Alertas Rojas al Analizar el Cierre Fiscal 2014, December 12, 2014.

[63] On September 30, 2014, El Salvador and the MCC signed a $277 million compact focused on improving education and human capital, improving the country's investment climate, and building logistical infrastructure. The U.S. investment is to be complemented by $88 million from the Salvadoran government and by private financing.

[64] Testimony of Mark Lopes, Deputy Assistant Administrator for Latin America and the Caribbean, USAID, before the House Committee on Foreign Affairs, Subcommittee on the Western Hemisphere, Children Migrating from Central America: Creating a Humanitarian Crisis, 113th Cong., 2nd sess., June 24, 2014.

[65] Jose Luis Sanz, "Guatemala: The Fall of Paz y Paz, the End of a Judicial Awakening," Insight Crime, August 15, 2014.

[66] Governments of El Salvador, Guatemala, and Honduras, Plan of the Alliance for Prosperity in the Northern Triangle: A Road Map, September 2014, http://idbdocs.iadb.org/wsdocs/getdocument. aspx? docnum =39224238.

[67] Michael McDonald, "Slowing Migrants to U.S. Will Cost $15 Billion, Guatemala Says," Bloomberg, January 26, 2015.

[68] CRS Report R42917, Mexico: Background and U.S. Relations, by Clare Ribando Seelke. For historical background, see CRS Report R42560, Mexican Migration to the United States: Policy and Trends, coordinated by Ruth Ellen Wasem.

[69] Jeffrey Passel, D'Vera Cohn, and Ana Gonzalez-Barrera, Net Migration from Mexico Falls to Zero—And Perhaps Less, Pew Hispanic Center, Washington, DC, 2012.

[70] White House, Office of the Press Secretary, "Remarks by President Obama and President Peña Nieto after Bilateral Meeting," press release, January 6, 2015.

[71] Tracy Wilkinson, "Exploitation Awaits Migrant Children on Mexico's Southern Edge," Los Angeles Times, August 2, 2014.

[72] Reforms that migration experts have recommended include raising hiring standards for immigration agents, regulating how migrants should be treated, and strengthening internal and external controls over migration agents. Sonja Wolf et al., Assessment of the National Migration Institute: Towards an Accountability System for Migrant Rights in Mexico, INSYDE, 2014.

[73] Gobierno de Mexico, Sistema Institucional de Información Estadística (SIIE), "Incidencia Delictiva del Fuero Federal, 2014."

[74] For more information, see CRS Report R43001, Supporting Criminal Justice System Reform in Mexico: The U.S. Role, by Clare Ribando Seelke.

[75] Gabriel Stargardter and Patricia Zengerle, "E-Coyotes: The Central American People Smugglers Who 'Like' Facebook," Reuters, August 5, 2014; Oscar Martínez, "The Northern Triangle Children Don't Leave Alone: They Are Taken," Insight Crime, July 16, 2014.

[76] DHS, Bureau of Immigration and Customs Enforcement (ICE), "Fact Sheet: Human Trafficking and Smuggling," January 16, 2013.

[77] Chloe Gilroy and Sarah Kinosian, "U.S.-Mexico Border Security: Helping or Hurting Human Smuggling Networks," Security Assistance Monitor, August 12, 2014.

[78] White House, Office of the Vice President, "Remarks to the Press with Q&A by Vice President Joe Biden in Guatemala," press release, June 20, 2014.

[79] Eduardo Castillo and Christopher Sherman, "Migration Spotlights Mexican 'Coyote' Smugglers," Houston Chronicle, July 21, 2014.

[80] Oscar Martínez, "How the Zetas Tamed Central America's 'Coyotes'," Insight Crime, May 1, 2014.

[81] Gobierno de México, Secretaría de Gobernación (SEGOB), Estadística Migratoría- Síntesis 2014, December 2014.

[82] INM data as presented in electronic correspondence from the Mexican Embassy in Washington, DC, July 21, 2014.

[83] SEGOB, Respuesta a solicitud de información del Servicio de Investigación.

[84] SEGOB, 2014, op. cit.

[85] U.S. Department of State, Bureau of International Narcotics and Law Enforcement Affairs, "INL Assistance for Mexico's Southern Border Strategy," fact sheet, June 2014. For more information, see CRS Report R41349, U.S.- Mexican Security Cooperation: The Mérida Initiative and Beyond, by Clare Ribando Seelke and Kristin Finklea.

[86] U.N. Office for the Coordination of Humanitarian Assistance, Central America and Mexico: Unaccompanied Child Migration, Situation Report No. 01 (as of 29 July 2014.)

[87] U.N. Office for the Coordination of Humanitarian Assistance, "Central America and Mexico: Unaccompanied Child Migration," Situation Report No. 01 (as of 29 July 2014); U.N. High Commissioner for Refugees, "Central America and Mexico: UNHCR Regional Update," December 2014.

[88] U.N. High Commissioner for Refugees, "30th Commemorative Anniversary of the Cartagena Declaration on Refugees," December 2014.

[89] Anastasia Moloney, "Deported Central America Child Migrants Face Threats, Death at Home – UN – TRFN," Reuters, February 3, 2015.

[90] See, for example, Otto Pérez Molina, "In Latin America, We Know Who Is to Blame for Our Child Migrant Crisis," Guardian, August 2, 2014; and General John F. Kelly, "SOUTHCOM Chief: Central America Drug War a Dire Threat to U.S. National Security," Military Times, July 8, 2014.

[91] Testimony of Francisco Palmieri, Deputy Assistant Secretary for the Caribbean and Central America, U.S. Department of State, before the Senate Committee on Homeland Security and Governmental Affairs, Challenges at the Border: Examining the Causes, Consequences, and Responses to the Rise in Apprehensions at the Southern Border, 113th Cong., 2nd sess., July 9, 2014.

[92] Statement of Eric L. Olson, before the before the Senate Committee on Homeland Security and Governmental Affairs, Challenges at the Border: Examining and Addressing the Root Causes Behind the Rise in Apprehensions at the Southern Border, 113th Cong., 2nd sess., July 16, 2014; Adam Isacson, "Isacson: Immigration Crisis Is Product of Perfect Storm of Conditions in Central America," Fox News Latino, July 25, 2014; and Héctor Silva Avalos, "How to Stop the Surge of Migrant Children: Focus on Security Misses Bigger Problems," New York Times, July 8, 2014.

In: Unaccompanied Children from Central America ISBN: 978-1-63482-937-3
Editor: Veronica K. Quinn 

*Chapter 4*

# TESTIMONY OF ELIZABETH HOGAN, SENIOR DEPUTY ASSISTANT FOR LATIN AMERICA AND THE CARIBBEAN, USAID. HEARING ON "UNACCOMPANIED ALIEN CHILDREN: PRESSING THE ADMINISTRATION FOR A STRATEGY"*

Chairman Salmon, Ranking Member Sires, Members of the Subcommittee, thank you for the opportunity to share how the U.S. Agency for International Development (USAID) is responding to the challenge of unaccompanied minors migrating from El Salvador, Guatemala and Honduras to the U.S. border. Our response to this challenge is consistent with the U.S. policy to address underlying causes of this problem and our mission to partner to end extreme poverty and promote resilient, democratic societies while advancing our security and prosperity.

Through family connections, remittance flows, economic ties and gang activity, the countries of Central America are increasingly linked to communities in the United States, some of which are located just a few miles from this hearing room. For the past five years, USAID has worked alongside the State Department and other U.S. agencies to prioritize assistance in the areas of security, governance and economic development in Guatemala,

* This is an edited, reformatted and augmented version of testimony presented November 18, 2014 before the House Committee on Foreign Affairs, Subcommittee on the Western Hemisphere.

Honduras and El Salvador. In recognition of the gravity of the development challenges in Central America and the impact those challenges could have on the United States, USAID has maintained funding levels to Central America even in a constrained budget environment. In fact, we have shifted approximately $100 million over the last five years from USAID programs in South America to Central America.

Although we have shifted resources and maintained the budget, clearly more needs to be done. This is why the Administration requested additional resources in the FY 2014 supplemental budget request and why we look forward to working with Congress to ramp up our programming as additional resources become available. We believe these additional resources will result in security and development gains that exceed their costs – even in the short run, and most certainly in the medium to longer term. Our confidence in the effectiveness of our approach at the scale we have been able to enact is based on a recent independent impact evaluation in high crime communities in El Salvador, Guatemala, Honduras and Panama that provide statistically significant evidence that crime rates are lower and public perception of security higher in the areas in which we work as a direct result of our crime prevention efforts. Getting wider results on the ground that will impact the lives of millions of citizens, however, needs resources to scale up and nationalize these very positive efforts.

Mr. Chairman, we have learned that the reasons for migrations are varied and complex. For example, the child migrants from Guatemala are predominantly from indigenous communities and rural areas while those from Honduras are largely from urban areas. We know that the underlying factors of lack of economic opportunity, threats to personal security, and the wish to reunite with families coupled with misperceptions about U.S. immigration laws are driving migration, yet some of these factors weigh more heavily for some communities than others. Most of the young people arriving at the U.S.-Mexico border are between the ages of 14 and 17. Many of them are aware that the journey is dangerous. Nevertheless, they and their parents choose to take this risk, and many of them do so more than once.

The surge in unaccompanied minors migrating out of Central America makes the adoption, ownership and expansion of proven crime and violence prevention approaches by Central American governments more important than ever. Our greatest impact, over time, will be that programs which have demonstrated success become the policy of the host nation-supported by their taxpayers. We are heartened that these governments are increasingly dedicating additional financial and intellectual resources to address the root causes of violence and criminality in their countries. However, even greater investment by Central American governments is needed to deepen the impact of our joint efforts. Host nations are working hard to help their most vulnerable populations who live on the margins of the formal economy, but we can and should urge them to do more to enact needed reforms. As the Vice President told Central American leaders on November 14 at the Inter-American Development Bank conference on addressing the constraints to growth in El Salvador, Honduras and Guatemala, "Urgent challenges demand urgent action—backed by courage and political will. It's hard, but it can be done."

In terms of a direct response to this year's migration flow, USAID has moved quickly to strengthen the reception capacity of the three main countries of origin. Through a \$7.6M grant to the International Organization for Migration (IOM), we are working to ensure that countries can receive and process increased numbers of returnees of all ages. In addition, we are working to make sure that the governments in the region can provide any immediate care and onward assistance for returning families and children so that they are received home in a safe, dignified, and orderly manner.

Pending final Congressional approval, USAID expects to implement up to \$160 million in FY 2014 funds to tackle the root causes of the crime, violence and economic insecurity driving the child migration phenomenon. Through the Central America Regional Security Initiative (CARSI), we are supporting crime and violence prevention programs that expand opportunities for youth living in insecure neighborhoods and strengthen the institutions charged with administering justice and keeping people safe.

USAID's prevention strategy revolves around smart targeting – geographic, demographic, and according to a specific set of risk factors for violence. In simple terms, our work seeks to concentrate prevention efforts on high-risk youth in high-risk communities. For example, by partnering with the Los Angeles Mayor's Office and the University of Southern California, we are using tried and tested methodology to identify a set of specific risk factors most associated with youths joining gangs.

We have evidence that these kinds of programs are working, and evidence is crucial so we can build on what really works. The final results from a four-year, third-party impact evaluation carried out by Vanderbilt University in high crime communities in El Salvador, Guatemala, Honduras and Panama show that – as a direct result of USAID's programs – reported crime is lower and public perception of security higher. Our community-based crime prevention approach is a package of activities that include programs for at-risk youth, such as outreach centers that provide safe spaces and workforce preparedness training; security-related planning by municipal crime prevention committees; activities that address environmental issues like street lighting and graffiti; and community policing.

The Vanderbilt evaluation found that, compared to what would have occurred without USAID intervention, 57% fewer residents in targeted communities in Honduras reported being aware of extortion in their neighborhoods; in Guatemala, 60% fewer residents reported being aware of homicides in their neighborhoods; and in El Salvador, 36% fewer residents reported being aware of illegal drug sales in their neighborhoods. People believe and see their communities are getting better.

Agustin, a former gang member from Guatemala, participated in a USAID funded prevention program several years ago. He turned his life around, became a family man, and now gives "prevention talks" to schools in his community. As an activist with the Youth Movement Against Violence, Agustin has starred in his own Tedx Talk series offering solutions for at risk youth.

USAID is already starting to expand the most successful prevention approaches beyond the initial test communities, working with municipal and national Central American leaders. For instance, over the past six years, we have increased our network of youth outreach centers -- which offer youth services and refuge from gang violence -- from 25 in Guatemala to 139 across Central America, and worked with mayors to root these programs in the community. And we are preparing to open an additional 77 centers in high-crime neighborhoods in El Salvador. In Honduras alone, tens of thousands of youth have received assistance through more than 40 such centers based in that country's most violent cities. President Hernandez of Honduras has seen this in action and has publicly committed to allocating 30 percent of the funds collected through the country's Security Tax to support prevention programs.

In Guatemala, the government has expanded USAID's successful 24-hour court model to additional communities, demonstrating its commitment to an independent and accessible judicial system, and the Government of El Salvador launched its ambitious new National Strategy for Violence Prevention in February to empower municipalities to lead on prevention efforts.

Going forward, USAID will continue to better target our assistance to those communities where crime, violence and child migration rates remain high, working alongside the State Department, Departments of Justice and Homeland Security, and other international donors. Through the *Safer City* model, which we are currently developing, we will align our resources and efforts with those of host governments, donors, private sector, and multi-laterals to ensure economies of scale. The most effective way to reduce homicide and violence is through such an integrated approach, which must ultimately be scaled up by the governments in the region.

While insecurity related to crime and violence is cited as a primary driver for the migration of minors from the region, the lack of jobs and economic opportunities at home for youth and their families is also a crucial factor. USAID's development programs -- to create jobs, spur agricultural development, strengthen food security and improve literacy and youth workforce development -- seek to improve the educational opportunities and livelihoods for the poor in more rural areas. These programs remain particularly relevant because they complement and amplify our youth and urban-oriented CARSI programming and will be coordinated with our outreach efforts with the private sector. As Secretary of Commerce Pritzker told the presidents of El Salvador, Honduras and Guatemala on November 14, "to further advance your countries' success, we want to see your best and brightest young people stay home, start businesses, and help grow your economies."

In Guatemala, for instance, USAID is investing nearly $25 million over five years in a new program to improve educational access and quality for under-served populations, including rural indigenous girls and boys in 900 rural schools, and educational and vocational training opportunities for 2,000 out-of-school youth in the country's Western Highland region.

In El Salvador, where small and medium-enterprises (SMEs) account for half of all economic activity in a nation of 6 million people, a USAID partnership with Banco Davivienda unlocked $25 million for SMEs to help spur job creation.

As part of our Feed the Future investments in Honduras, USAID contributed $24.5 million to the new Dry Corridor Initiative to promote sustainable agricultural development in the country's drought-plagued southwest border region and improve the livelihoods of some 50,000 families.

And we are supporting a robust program across the region to limit the devastation of the Coffee Rust epidemic on Central America's lucrative coffee sector. Our investments are helping small-scale coffee growers and workers all along the coffee value chain replant, refinance and improve management of coffee farms.

These kinds of economic development programs align with our crime prevention programs to build a foundation for prosperous economies that offer economic and other opportunities for youth and their families, and in so doing relieve the pressure to migrate north. The integrated nature of our assistance in Central America is precisely why we are not looking to cut programs in rural agriculture or climate change or health and redirect those resources exclusively to crime prevention programs. We caution against narrowing our portfolio in those countries any further.

The U.S. government continues to successfully utilize partnerships with the private sector to supplement and sustain our investments in Central America and encourage corporate social responsibility. Over the past few years, USAID has leveraged approximately $40 million in private sector resources to support at-risk youth. For example, through a USAID and Microsoft collaboration in El Salvador, approximately 25,000 youth in 13 high-crime municipalities will have access to competitive computer and technology training and a path to certification. These partnerships are part of an effort to help build a Central American economy that provides viable opportunities for current and future generations to thrive.

Such partnerships are also integral to the effectiveness of our economic development programs. In Honduras alone, USAID has developed 41 partnerships with companies, including Syngenta and Walmart, to strengthen key agricultural value chains and increase incomes of farmers and agricultural workers (more than 24,000 to date). We're also partnering with coffee industry leaders, Keurig Green Mountain, Starbucks and Smuckers, to help coffee farming areas recover from the coffee rust outbreak.

The U.S. strategy in Central America recognizes the inextricable requirements of progress in areas of prosperity, security and governance. We remain convinced that only by working to keep children safe and in school, train out-of-school youth for higher education or work and help business create jobs, while encouraging more government transparency, effectiveness and a stronger rule of law, will Central America become the peaceful and prosperous region we all desire.

Thank you and I look forward to answering any questions you may have.

In: Unaccompanied Children from Central America ISBN: 978-1-63482-937-3
Editor: Veronica K. Quinn 

*Chapter 5*

# TESTIMONY OF ROBERTA S. JACOBSON, ASSISTANT SECRETARY OF STATE, BUREAU OF WESTERN HEMISPHERE AFFAIRS, U.S. DEPARTMENT OF STATE. HEARING ON "UNACCOMPANIED ALIEN CHILDREN: PRESSING THE ADMINISTRATION FOR A STRATEGY"*

Mr. Chairman, Ranking Member Sires, and Members of the Committee:

Thank you for the opportunity to testify on the United States strategy for engagement with Central America. I know many of you have been personally involved on this issue. The Administration welcomes the support and interest of this committee in our efforts to develop a humane and effective response to these migrants – unaccompanied children and families – arriving at our southwest border. Although we are encouraged that the numbers have decreased since July, we remain vigilant in our efforts to protect these children and address the underlying factors of violence and poverty in their countries of origin that are pushing them north.

More than sixty-five thousand unaccompanied children have left their homes to make the dangerous journey to the United States this year. From a

* This is an edited, reformatted and augmented version of testimony presented November 18, 2014 before the House Committee on Foreign Affairs, Subcommittee on the Western Hemisphere.

foreign policy perspective, this migration is a warning sign that the serious and longstanding challenges in Central America are worsening. The course of action is clear. We must adequately address the underlying factors compelling so many to undertake this dangerous journey or be prepared for what is likely to be an ongoing cyclical phenomenon - with significant cost to the United States.

A stable, prosperous, and well-governed Central America is an important national security interest of the United States. Just last week, the Inter-American Development Bank hosted a conference on "Investing in Central America" where Vice President Biden and the Presidents from El Salvador, Guatemala, and Honduras spoke about opportunities and challenges for growth and better governance in Central America. We appreciate the IDB's role in bringing stakeholders together and offering to provide follow-up technical meetings.

Fortunately, we believe the essential condition for finding solutions is present: political will in the region. Central American leaders recognize the scope of the challenges they face at home and have begun to act. At the IDB conference, the presidents of El Salvador, Guatemala, and Honduras publicly presented an unprecedented, coordinated plan – the Alliance for Prosperity in the Northern Triangle. Their plan includes a clear-eyed assessment of the region's challenges, well-considered lines of action to resolve them, and specific priorities that they themselves will pursue. The plan addresses the underlying factors of migration and promotes a region of opportunity for all of its citizens, especially young people. The presidents' message at the conference was simple: the region's leaders know they have serious challenges and are prepared to make the tough choices to address them, but they need our assistance.

Their agreement to a joint plan is, in and of itself, an important demonstration of this political will, which we must now harness to cultivate, and where appropriate, expand the effective developmental and security partnerships that are in the U.S. national interest.

Without significant progress in Central America, the region will continue to face extreme violence, severe economic inequality and social exclusion, and widespread corruption and poverty, compelling many Central Americans to flee their homes each year. Others will embark on this journey to reunify with relatives and family members who are already residing in the United States or to enjoy higher quality of life in the United States. A secure, democratic, and prosperous Central American region will be a stronger partner for the United

States and will provide an environment in which all of its citizens, including youth, find opportunities to build their lives at home.

Over the course of the past 18 months, the U.S. government has taken a hard look at both our approach and our investments. We determined that while security is still paramount, in order to succeed, we needed to broaden our vision. Consequently, we developed an interagency strategy that can support much of what the leaders of Central America put forward in their own coordinated plan. The U.S. Strategy for Engagement with Central America both aligns with and supports the objectives of the Alliance for Prosperity plan.

To achieve this vision, U.S. engagement with Central America must balance three objectives prosperity, governance, and security. These goals are interrelated and interdependent.

Our *prosperity* agenda fosters integration of a regional market of 43 million people so that local businesses can become more competitive and the region can be more attractive to international investors. *Economic growth should reach everyone, not just the well-connected few.* Our efforts will promote better education and vocational training for all citizens including women and vulnerable ethnic groups, and create business environments that are friendly to entrepreneurs, and provide alternatives to the illicit activities that contribute to insecurity and undermine effective governance.

Our *governance* agenda recognizes that *economic growth is only sustainable when the rule of law and democratic institutions flourish, corruption and impunity is reduced, fundamental freedoms are respected, and civil society and the media can play their rightful roles.* In many Central American countries, citizens, businesses and governments face corruption, transnational crime, and political cronyism. In such an environment, governments often fail to provide the most basic services and protections. We know that the sustainability of U.S. efforts will be magnified if we focus on government effectiveness and accountability, and leverage our investments to demand honest leadership and a verifiable commitment to the rule of law from our partners in the region.

Without a doubt, *the security agenda will remain a core priority*. If we do not collectively and effectively address insecurity now from neighborhood streets to transnational criminal networks in El Salvador, Guatemala, and Honduras, the payoff from our other important investments will not bear fruit in the longer term.

Let me be clear. We are still a long way from achieving our core goals of sustained prosperity, good governance, and security in Central America. There is no greater indication of this fact than what we all witnessed this past summer: the willingness of tens of thousands of children to abandon their homes and travel up the isthmus and through Mexico to the United States – at substantial cost and amid the ever-present risk of rape, abuse, and death – to flee the dire conditions many face in their home communities.

Mr. Chairman, I can report that over the past few months, in partnership with Central American governments, we have achieved several important successes. Our coordinated public messaging campaigns informed families about the dangers of a migrant's journey effectively and countered false messages peddled by migrant smugglers. Increased focus on smuggling networks in Honduras and Guatemala by host country law enforcement, including U.S. trained and vetted teams, has led to arrests of smugglers and the rescue of over 235 children. El Salvador, Guatemala, and Honduras are all regularly receiving repatriation flights. The Government of Mexico has also been a vital partner.

While historical migration trends typically show a decrease in the number of migrants crossing the U.S. southern border during the hot summer months and in the fall, we believe that unprecedented efforts on the part of the Administration and our partners in Central America and Mexico bore meaningful results. The number of unaccompanied children apprehended at the U.S.-Mexico border decreased from 10,628 in June to 2,514 in October – levels last seen in January 2013.

As interdiction and enforcement efforts ramp up, we remain conscious of the need to provide protection for children and other vulnerable migrants who need it—and this too is a central component of our efforts.

Our colleagues in the State Department's Bureau of Population, Refugees and Migration – or PRM – are working with international organizations, like the Office of the United Nations High Commissioner for Refugees (UNHCR), to strengthen asylum systems in the region and find ways to protect children who are threatened or displaced in their own countries so they are not forced to flee. They support the International Organization for Migration (TOM) to help the region's governments manage migration and enforce border security in a humane way. At the direction of the White House, PRM has also worked with the Department of Homeland Security, US Citizenship and Immigration Service (USCIS) to develop a new program that was announced by Vice President Biden in his remarks last week at the Inter-American Development Bank. This new program will allow parents lawfully present in the United States to petition for their children in El Salvador, Guatemala, and Honduras to come to the United States as refugees. Those children not eligible for refugee status will be considered on a case-by-case basis for humanitarian parole. Our aim is to offer a safe, legal, and orderly alternative to a child making the dangerous journey alone to the US border.

However, any progress cannot be sustained without an increased and re-engaged U.S. commitment to our long-term strategy in Central America. We assess that it could take $5 billion over 5 years to fully implement this strategy. It is our intent to work with our regional partners who are going to put their own money and expertise into the effort, coordinate more effectively with international financial institutions, and promote private sector leadership in their efforts on this issue. Our own contributions will leverage these efforts and demonstrate American leadership and commitment to the region.

Despite serious and complex challenges, there is reason to be optimistic about Central America's future. As I mentioned, I believe the three leaders of the Northern Triangle countries of El Salvador, Guatemala, and Honduras are prepared to make hard decisions and to invest their own national budgets. Leaders in Panama and Costa Rica are demonstrating how the region can modernize and integrate to achieve better economic outcomes. Now is the time for a new U.S. approach to Central America that harnesses the region's political will for change and advances a strategy that balances and prioritizes prosperity, good governance, and security in equal measure. We have a vision, we have a plan, and we want to work with Congress to help Central America and protect U.S. national security.

Thank you and I welcome your questions.

In: Unaccompanied Children from Central America ISBN: 978-1-63482-937-3
Editor: Veronica K. Quinn 

*Chapter 6*

# TESTIMONY OF ROBERT N. KAPLAN, PRESIDENT AND CEO, INTER-AMERICAN FOUNDATION. HEARING ON "UNACCOMPANIED ALIEN CHILDREN: PRESSING THE ADMINISTRATION FOR A STRATEGY"*

Chairman Salmon, Ranking Member Sires and members of the Subcommittee:

Thank you for the opportunity to appear today to testify on behalf of the Inter-American Foundation (IAF), a small independent foreign assistance agency of the U.S. government that works directly with the organized poor in Latin America and the Caribbean. The board and staff of the IAF appreciate this Subcommittee's long-standing support for our mission of promoting and investing in citizen-led grassroots development to help communities thrive.

As the members of this Subcommittee deliberate on weighty matters of national and regional scope in our hemisphere, we appreciate your interest in a community-level perspective. We all know from our own country's experience that thriving communities strengthen democracy, expand economic opportunities and enhance social resilience. Our strongest communities are

* This is an edited, reformatted and augmented version of testimony presented November 18, 2014 before the House Committee on Foreign Affairs, Subcommittee on the Western Hemisphere.

those where ordinary citizens work together as neighbors to achieve common objectives. That is the essence of the IAF's work in Latin America and the Caribbean. I am pleased to discuss with you today our activities in Central America, and how we can complement the efforts of other government agencies, as well as private organizations and firms, to help our Central American neighbors provide better opportunities for their citizens to lead healthy, safe and productive lives.

You well know the long list of "push" factors in Central America that contribute to individuals' decisions to leave their community. Regardless of whether they move to another part of their country, to somewhere else in Central America or Mexico, or attempt to cross into the United States, the exodus is a symptom that something is wrong back home.

In poor communities where the IAF works, we see the human costs of too few good jobs, barriers to starting and sustaining small enterprises, and a lack of viable options for young people to continue their education locally. Access to clean water, basic utilities, good roads and affordable sources of energy are often scarce. In the "northern triangle" of El Salvador, Guatemala and Honduras, one-quarter of the population subsists on less than $2.00 per day. How can parents send their children to high school in a neighboring town when gangs routinely board buses to shake down students, or worse? The cost of extortion keeps entrepreneurs from opening shops. Neighborhoods divided by gangs or at-risk from organized crime shutter at 7:00 p.m. When natural disasters strike, the poor are particularly vulnerable. This year's severe drought in Central America added to the misery in rural communities already suffering from the devastating effects of a widespread outbreak of coffee rust. Small farmers have reported losing half their crop.

Facing these threats, families do not know where to turn. Government institutions are too often absent, unable to respond adequately or simply not trusted. When citizens feel unprotected by the state, it is little wonder that they lose faith that democracy can work for them. Community "safety nets" have broken down as well; local civil society organizations are under-resourced and themselves subject to many of the same pressures, vulnerabilities and fears. The private sector can do more to provide a spark for economic development that is inclusive and benefits local people most likely to migrate. But too often, reports of corruption and firms' indifference to the local population fuel cynicism and contribute to a climate of despair.

It is in this context that the IAF has invested carefully over many years to help local Central American citizens' organizations gain some control over their lives by carrying out initiatives that they themselves conceive. Our partners set priorities and demonstrate their commitment by contributing their own funds to the effort; on average, they provide about $1.30 for every $1.00 invested by the IAF, making the U.S. a minority partner in the development projects we support. Our portfolio is diverse because it reflects local priorities, ranging from microbusiness development to agricultural diversification to domestic violence prevention to watershed management. At the same time, our selection process ensures that we apply our resources prudently to achieve U.S. interests as well. As others invest in improving state institutions, the IAF invests directly at the grassroots to strengthen the capacity of citizens to be protagonists in their communities' development and to engage their governments effectively.

Today, our active portfolio in Central America includes 81 projects, representing $37 million of combined investment by the IAF and our grantee partners. Looking only at the three northern triangle countries, we are supporting local initiatives in over 880 communities. Similarly, in Mexico, we are supporting work in over 400 communities, mostly in the southern states. These urban and rural communities are the homes of families struggling to sustain and protect themselves.

What are some of the results of the IAF's investments? Our grantee partners report their results every six months, and we independently verify the information. In the last few years, they created over 14,300 new jobs for low-income people in Central America. In the northern triangle, 80 percent of our grantee partners who tracked income generation reported an increase, on average more than doubling household income in a year.

Participation has changed the appeal of migration. In a survey of participants in one project that helped create 15 community-based businesses in El Salvador, less than 22 percent of those aged 25 years or younger said they would consider migrating, compared to 83 percent when the project started. Most insist they want to contribute to the economic stability of their communities and create employment opportunities for their neighbors. Similarly, a recent IAF grantee partner in rural Guatemala used a combination of education programs on the risks of migration, credit and training for small farming businesses to reduce emigration among youth. Nearly 60 percent of families in this municipality had at least one member living in the United States, yet 79 percent of the 730 young participants had decided not to migrate by the end of the grant period.

Importantly, with half of Central America's population under 25 years old and a disproportionate number of them poor, many of the initiatives we support engage young people, and these are the focus of my remarks today.

About 45 percent of the IAF's investment in El Salvador, Guatemala and Honduras benefit young people directly; even more benefit indirectly as the children of mothers and fathers involved in IAF-funded programs.

What do we see that works to keep Central American youths in their home communities? Let me share a few insights from our experience.

Creating jobs by itself may not necessarily be enough to stem emigration. Similarly, providing activities to "occupy the time" of so-called "ni-ni's" -- a term referring to the one-quarter of youths aged 15-24 in Central America who neither study nor work -- is not sufficient if youths remain passive recipients of programs designed or carried out by others. A first lesson from our experience is that when disadvantaged youths come together on their own initiative to build skills and safe spaces, start their own small businesses, and exercise leadership and teamwork for the benefit of their community, they are less likely to leave. Why? Because they become *invested* in the *present* and *future* of their home communities. Through their own effort, young people with financial hardship acquire the tools, knowledge, confidence and social support networks that make it possible -- and preferable -- to sustain themselves in their home communities and respond constructively to crises. Ideally, their enthusiasm becomes contagious among their peers as well. As one Honduran teenager participating in an IAF-funded project in Tegucigalpa recently told us, *"Before participating in the program, I wanted only to follow the American Dream; now I believe that I can create my American Dream here."* And as a Salvadoran youth participant explained, *"Before, I thought of moving to a different country, but now I think about making changes in my country."*

Second, community-based initiatives should target those at greatest risk of migrating. This is a dynamic group of young people, who, though poor or disadvantaged, have impressive drive and ambition for their future and feel locked out of opportunities at home. Our grantee partners seek to unlock access to economic, educational and other social advancement in hundreds of communities where these young people live.

Third, it is important to let youths lead. Listen and respond to the ideas marginalized young people themselves present. Rather than treating them as passive participants or trainees, we need to give young people opportunities to take on leadership roles in the design, implementation and long-term sustainability of community-based initiatives.

Fourth, invest in both urban and rural youth, and meet them where they are -- in their home communities -- because it can be too dangerous for young people to travel outside of their neighborhoods. Central American youth migrants come from both urban and rural settings. In many cases, those from the countryside first migrate to city slums before eventually leaving the country. We have aligned our investments in the region to address this important dynamic.

Fifth, markets matter, and investing in the creation and improvement of local economic opportunities is fundamental. Young people need the skills to increase their competitiveness in the job market or to open and sustain small businesses. If they decide to go into business, they need access to affordable financing. With a poorly functioning economy that is unable to generate dignified work in so many communities, it is no surprise that the IAF receives so many requests to support microenterprise development, microcredit or community savings and loan associations.

Let me give you an example to illustrate this point. In the slums of Tegucigalpa and surrounding rural areas, IAF grantee partner Centro de Educación Vocacional Grupo Juvenil Dion (GJD) is working to improve the employment prospects of high-risk youths through vocational training, internships with local businesses and access to microcredit. A majority of the youth and their families live in areas of the city saturated with gang activity, poverty, and crime. The center combines training in hard skills with programs that develop communication and soft skills. So far, 800 young Hondurans have graduated with certification in technical trades and 105 have gotten access to microcredit to launch enterprises, including beauty salons, bakeries and carpentry businesses. At this point, 91 percent of borrowers are current with their loan payments. Importantly, “mobile workshops” take the training program to youths in communities outside metropolitan Tegucigalpa. Its marketing center provides a venue and support for six brands for the entrepreneurs’ products and services.

Sixth, building the ability of citizens to engage their government regarding urgent local needs is a critical step to increase their commitment to their home communities. Civic engagement is a challenge for marginalized communities with large out-migration. Many do not know how to raise concerns with their government and hold local officials to account for responding to citizens’ needs. Feeling hopeless about the ability to change their circumstances at home, they vote with their feet. Let me give you another example. An IAF grantee partner, Asociación Para el Desarrollo Sostenible de la Juventud (ADESJU), is changing this attitude among the 750 participants in its network of 25 youth groups. ADESJU is based in Chiantla, a municipality in Guatemala’s Western Highlands, where 78 percent of the population lives in poverty or extreme poverty and three-quarters of the population is under age

30. Participants in the association's leadership and teamwork development programs took it upon themselves to develop a detailed proposal to the municipal government with recommendations for programs or services that would address the urgent needs of local youth.

What is the IAF's role in these efforts? Our work involves much more than sending dollars to the region, and the direct results of the projects we fund tell only part of the story. Our whole approach to selecting, accompanying and evaluating our grassroots partners is designed to strengthen their capabilities so that they can take on even bigger challenges. As we invest directly with incipient grassroots organizations, we help strengthen local talent and capacity to participate effectively in civic life. We also help them tap into existing civil society networks, including the family of IAF grassroots groups across the region, and connect organizations with common or complementary interests so that they can form new partnerships of their own. We want them to learn from each other and become leaders in their own communities. In the process, they create social and economic anchors at home and demonstrate their preference to stay. I am convinced that this is indeed what people want because I have heard it repeatedly in hundreds of conversations with parents and grandparents who look on with dismay as their children leave.

This may sound like painstaking and meticulous work. It is. But that does not mean that it cannot be undertaken on a larger scale. The IAF has many years of experience nurturing local capabilities, and we can tap into extensive networks of grassroots organizations throughout the region to draw new resources and energy into the effort from a variety of sources.

So where do we go from here?

There are many opportunities to do so much at the grassroots to address the causes of youth migration *before* they leave or once they are returned. The IAF sees considerable talent and capacity in Central American civil society to *manage* more resources to help youth and their communities open economic opportunities and work with their governments and business sector to respond to challenges of crime and violence. The impact of a single thriving community, an organized group of rural poor or an inspired young person in an urban slum may appear small, but they become the safe havens and incubators of change that inspire others. There remain untapped thousands of communities, tens of thousands of organized groups and hundreds of thousands of young people ready to step forward with solutions and what little resources they have. If reached, if empowered and if connected to each other, they are capable of generating the sea change so desperately needed in the region.

We believe it is important to put community members -- including young leaders -- in the driver's seat to best address local problems. Youth need to be engaged in more than job-training or extra-curricular activities. They need a chance to become citizens. Fundamentally, they are the ones who will need to change their communities and countries.

Forty-five years ago a small congressional delegation of members of this committee paid a visit to Central America, in part to examine the effectiveness of U.S. development efforts in the region. What they learned was not surprising: that true, long-lasting, meaningful change depends in large part on thriving communities -- communities that provide not only social and economic opportunities for the most marginalized but that are themselves foundations upon which future democracies can be built. One result from that trip was the creation of the Inter-American Foundation. We are driven by the vision of thriving communities where people direct their own lives as individuals and citizens. Over our history we have supported more than 5,000 organizations in communities across the hemisphere in pursuit of this goal. While our grantee partners may be poor, they are not passive. When we are successful, they are protagonists – not participants -- with aspirations and the ability to think beyond a project and shape their own future.

Working at the community level as we do complements U.S. diplomatic efforts and other bilateral foreign assistance for improved prosperity, governance and security in Central American countries. Importantly, it serves Congress's intent in the creation of the Inter-American Foundation spelled out in our enabling legislation: to "*strengthen the bonds of friendship and understanding among the peoples of this hemisphere*."

Again, I thank the Subcommittee for the opportunity to testify before you today on behalf of the IAF and our thousands of grassroots partners in the region.

# INDEX

## A

abuse, 7, 78
access, 5, 6, 9, 57, 60, 73, 74, 84, 85
accountability, 77
adults, 53
advancement, 84
age, 20, 23, 24, 27, 28, 30, 32, 33, 63, 85
agencies, 2, 3, 4, 5, 10, 11, 17, 18, 19, 21, 33, 42, 48, 53, 57, 60, 61, 69, 82
agriculture, 42, 74
AIDS, 42
Air Force, 52, 53
alien smuggling, 57, 58
ambassadors, 4, 19
appropriations, 36, 42, 46, 47, 48, 59, 62, 63
Appropriations Act, 42, 47
armed conflict, 55
arrest(s), 46, 58, 78
assessment, 11, 76
asylum, 33, 38, 40, 52, 59, 60, 61, 62, 78
Attorney General, 53, 56
audit, 4, 20
authorities, 35, 60
awareness, 45

## B

banking, 53
banks, 55
barriers, 82
base, 53
basic education, 16, 42
basic services, 77
benchmarks, 47
benefits, 82
*Bilateral*, 67
bilateral aid, 49
blind spot, 12
bonds, 87
Border Patrol, 18, 33, 37
border security, 47, 48, 58, 59, 78
borrowers, 85
Brazil, 62
business costs, 42
business environment, 48, 77
businesses, 16, 73, 77, 83, 85

## C

campaigns, 46, 48, 62, 78
capacity building, 47
Caribbean, v, 40, 61, 62, 66, 67, 68, 69, 81, 82
CARSI, 1, 4, 5, 42, 43, 47, 49, 50, 51, 64, 71, 73
CBP, vii, 1, 3, 18, 24, 26, 33, 37, 45, 65
Census, 65

Central America Regional Security Initiative, 1, 4, 33, 42, 43, 64, 66, 71
certification, 74, 85
challenges, vii, 2, 4, 18, 41, 55, 63, 70, 71, 76, 79, 86
child development, 5
child protection, 46, 53, 54
childhood, 5
cities, 3, 11, 14, 72
citizens, 43, 52, 77, 82, 83, 85
citizenship, 7, 8
City, 9, 53, 72
civic life, 86
civil service, 49
civil service reform, 49
civil society, 2, 10, 11, 49, 54, 57, 63, 77, 82, 86
clean energy, 41
clients, 58
climate, 43, 67, 74, 82
climate change, 74
coastal region, 56
coding, 20
coercion, 58
coffee, 6, 12, 73, 74, 82
Cold War, 40
collaboration, 42, 64, 74
communication, 66, 85
communities, 3, 9, 10, 11, 12, 14, 18, 47, 53, 61, 69, 70, 71, 72, 78, 81, 82, 83, 84, 85, 86, 87
community, 10, 18, 35, 38, 47, 48, 54, 56, 71, 72, 81, 82, 83, 84, 85, 86, 87
competitiveness, 85
complement, 73, 82
complexity, 37
computer, 74
conference, 45, 71, 76
conflict, 12, 60, 66
Congress, 23, 33, 34, 35, 36, 38, 39, 45, 46, 47, 48, 51, 59, 63, 64, 66, 70, 79, 87
consensus, 38
consent, 58
construction, 53
conversations, 86
conviction, 58
cooperation, 16, 36, 43, 61
corruption, 20, 43, 55, 58, 63, 66, 76, 77, 82
cost, 76, 78, 82
Costa Rica, 5, 42, 51, 79
counseling, 8
country of origin, 60
crimes, 58
criminal activity, 5, 58, 60
criminal justice system, 55, 56, 58
criminality, 71
crises, 8, 66, 84
cronyism, 77
crop, 6, 82
Customs and Border Protection, vii, 1, 3, 24, 33, 37, 45, 64

## D

database, 18
deficiencies, 43
democracy, 81, 82
Department of Defense, 60
Department of Health and Human Services, 24
Department of Homeland Security, 1, 2, 3, 13, 15, 19, 24, 33, 44, 45, 65, 78
Department of Justice, 33, 46
despair, 82
detention, 60, 61
developing nations, 43
DHS, vii, 1, 2, 3, 4, 6, 7, 8, 9, 10, 11, 12, 13, 14, 15, 17, 18, 19, 24, 27, 44, 45, 46, 52, 65, 66, 68
dignity, 60
diplomacy, 45
diplomatic efforts, 87
diplomatic engagement, 15
direct investment, 44
directives, 48
directors, 4, 19
disadvantaged youth, 84
displaced persons, 51, 62
displacement, 52, 60, 61
distribution, 29

diversification, 83
diversity, 38
DOJ, 46
domestic policy, 64
domestic violence, 7, 9, 83
Dominican Republic, 36, 43, 65
donors, 52, 72
draft, 13, 15, 18
drawing, 2, 6
drought, 73, 82
drug trafficking, 6
drugs, 8
duty-free access, 40

## E

earthquakes, 44
economic activity, 16, 73
economic assistance, 43
economic crisis, 8
economic development, 3, 69, 73, 74, 82
economic growth, 9, 16, 20, 55, 64, 77
economic growth rate, 55
economic reform(s), 41, 42
economies of scale, 73
education, 5, 6, 14, 16, 43, 48, 54, 56, 60, 67, 77, 82, 83
educational opportunities, 13, 14, 16, 20, 73
educational system, 5, 7
electricity, 48
eligibility criteria, 20
embassy, 3, 15, 17
emergency, 46, 54
emigration, 56, 57, 83, 84
employment, 53, 54, 83, 85
employment opportunities, 83
energy, 57, 82, 86
enforcement, 33, 45, 57, 58, 78
entrepreneurs, 16, 77, 82, 85
environment, 70, 77
environmental issues, 72
epidemic, 73
equipment, 43, 52, 59
ethnic groups, 77
evidence, 4, 20, 33, 70, 71
executive branch, 15
exercise, 84
expertise, 79
exports, 44
extreme poverty, 16, 69, 85

## F

Facebook, 67
faith, 82
families, 2, 7, 8, 33, 46, 48, 53, 54, 56, 60, 61, 70, 71, 73, 74, 75, 78, 82, 83, 85
family members, 7, 10, 38, 54, 76
farmers, 74, 82
farms, 73
fear(s), 56, 60, 82
Federal Register, 66
female rat, 30
financial, 5, 43, 49, 70, 84
firearms, 55
flights, 78
focus groups, 10, 11
food, 53, 60, 73
food security, 73
force, 17, 44, 58
foreign aid, 41
foreign assistance, 36, 41, 48, 81, 87
foreign investment, 55
foreign nationals, 63
foreign policy, 36, 38, 45, 51, 76
foreign-born population, 44
foundations, 87
France, 66
fraud, 58
freedom, 43
friendship, 87
funding, 13, 14, 20, 36, 41, 42, 43, 46, 47, 48, 49, 51, 52, 59, 63, 70
funds, 5, 11, 36, 42, 47, 48, 49, 56, 71, 72, 83
fungus, 6, 12

## G


gangs, 6, 9, 71, 82
GAO, 1, 2, 13, 15, 21
GDP, 56, 67
geography, 18
GHP, 50, 51
governance, 9, 36, 41, 43, 46, 49, 55, 56, 63, 69, 74, 76, 77, 79, 87
governments, 3, 17, 36, 40, 45, 46, 48, 49, 52, 54, 55, 56, 60, 61, 62, 70, 71, 73, 77, 78, 83, 86
graffiti, 72
grassroots, 81, 83, 86, 87
gravity, 70
gross domestic product, 56
growth, 16, 27, 71, 76, 77
guardian, 20, 24, 27, 53, 63


## H


harmonization, 42
health, 5, 9, 42, 49, 74
health care, 5
health services, 9
hemisphere, 41, 81, 87
HHS, 24, 66
high school, 82
higher education, 74
Highlands, 9, 12, 14, 16, 85
highways, 58
hiring, 67
history, 87
Homeland Security Act, 33, 34
homes, 35, 38, 75, 76, 78, 83
homicide, 4, 10, 73
homicide rates, 4
hopelessness, 8
host, 2, 3, 10, 11, 15, 17, 70, 73, 78
House, 47, 67, 69, 75, 81
household income, 83
housing, 5
human, 5, 7, 13, 40, 43, 46, 47, 57, 58, 60, 67, 82
human capital, 5, 43, 67
human right(s), 40, 60
humanitarian organizations, 61
hygiene, 53, 54


## I


identification, 17, 53
IMF, 67
immigrants, 45
immigration, 6, 8, 12, 13, 14, 20, 23, 24, 26, 28, 33, 38, 44, 45, 57, 58, 67
Immigration and Customs Enforcement (ICE), 65, 66, 68
imports, 44
improvements, 54, 62, 63
income, 5, 6, 9, 56, 64, 67, 83
income inequality, 5
independence, 47
individuals, 9, 38, 51, 53, 56, 58, 59, 61, 62, 82, 87
industry, 74
inequality, 55, 56, 76
infrastructure, 14, 24, 43, 52, 56, 57, 67
insecurity, 36, 55, 56, 71, 73, 77
inspections, 33
institutional reforms, 55
institutions, 36, 41, 42, 43, 48, 49, 52, 55, 56, 57, 59, 63, 71, 77, 82, 83
integration, 42, 48, 77
intelligence, 10
Inter-American Development Bank, 45, 56, 67, 71, 76, 78
internally displaced, 52
international financial institutions, 79
International Monetary Fund, 67
International Narcotics Control, 51, 66
International Rescue Committee, 61
intervention, 72
investment(s), 5, 43, 67, 71, 73, 74, 77, 83, 84, 85
investors, 77
issues, 2, 3, 4, 9, 10, 15, 16, 19, 20, 23, 24, 33, 36, 38, 42, 51, 55, 61

## J


job creation, 73
job training, 54
job training programs, 54


## L


labor market, 43
language barrier, 18
languages, 18
Latin America, i, ii, iii, v, 41, 61, 62, 64, 66, 67, 68, 69, 81, 82
law enforcement, 5, 43, 48, 57, 78
laws, 33, 57
lead, 8, 58, 61, 72, 82, 84
leadership, 62, 77, 79, 84, 86
learning, 14
legislation, 36, 47, 87
literacy, 48, 73
local authorities, 52
local youth, 86
location information, 18
logistics, 5


## M


majority, vii, 2, 3, 9, 25, 29, 37, 40, 43, 49, 51, 85
man, 72
management, 5, 43, 49, 73, 83
mapping, 18, 61
market access, 44
marketing, 7, 10, 85
matter, 85
media, 45, 57, 77
median, 23, 27, 32
medical, 34, 53, 54, 60
medical care, 60
merchandise, 44
messages, 78
methodology, 71
metropolitan areas, 45
Mexican nationals, vii, 2, 3
Mexico, 34, 36, 37, 38, 39, 43, 46, 47, 51, 53, 57, 58, 59, 60, 64, 65, 67, 68, 70, 78, 82, 83
Miami, 66
Microsoft, 74
migrants, 2, 6, 7, 8, 9, 10, 11, 14, 17, 36, 38, 46, 47, 48, 57, 58, 60, 61, 62, 67, 70, 75, 78, 85
migration, vii, 2, 3, 4, 6, 7, 8, 9, 10, 11, 12, 13, 14, 15, 16, 17, 19, 20, 36, 39, 46, 47, 57, 58, 59, 61, 62, 67, 70, 71, 72, 73, 76, 78, 83, 85, 86
military, 49, 55
Ministry of Education, 16
minors, 7, 13, 14, 30, 34, 35, 36, 37, 38, 45, 47, 48, 51, 52, 53, 54, 58, 59, 63, 69, 70, 73
mission, vii, 2, 4, 11, 19, 47, 69, 81
*Multilateral*, 67


## N


narcotics, 43
national security, 76, 79
National Strategy, 72
nationality, 24, 33
natural disaster(s), 41, 56, 60, 66, 82
NGOs, 54, 60, 61
Nicaragua, 5, 42, 51
NRC, 62
nutrition, 5


## O


OAS, 61
Obama, 36, 41, 45, 46, 62, 64
Obama Administration, 36, 41, 45, 46, 62, 64
Office of the Inspector General, 33
officials, 2, 3, 4, 5, 6, 7, 8, 9, 10, 11, 13, 15, 16, 17, 18, 19, 20, 21, 28, 45, 51, 53, 58, 63, 85
operations, 46, 48, 62

opportunities, 3, 5, 12, 16, 36, 43, 49, 57, 62, 63, 71, 73, 74, 76, 77, 81, 84, 85, 86, 87
Organization of American States, 61
outreach, 12, 15, 45, 49, 72, 73
ownership, 70

## P

Panama, 5, 12, 14, 42, 51, 65, 70, 71, 79
parents, 5, 7, 23, 24, 58, 70, 78, 82, 86
parole, 5, 46, 79
participants, 11, 83, 84, 85, 87
penalties, 57
police, 8, 10, 16, 47, 55, 58
policy, 6, 8, 12, 13, 14, 35, 38, 39, 41, 57, 63, 70, 76
policy makers, 35, 38, 63
political crisis, 8
political system, 55
poor performance, 43
population, 5, 23, 30, 66, 82, 83, 85
portfolio, 74, 83
poverty, 5, 9, 16, 20, 38, 48, 55, 56, 60, 75, 76, 85
preparedness, 72
President, vi, 15, 42, 44, 45, 53, 57, 65, 67, 68, 72, 81
President Obama, 44, 45, 57, 67
prevention, 14, 43, 48, 56, 57, 61, 70, 71, 72, 73, 83
principles, 60
private sector, 43, 55, 73, 74, 79, 82
profit, 58
programming, 14, 17, 70, 73
project, 14, 54, 66, 83, 84, 87
prosperity, 36, 46, 48, 49, 69, 74, 77, 79, 87
protection, 37, 59, 60, 61, 62, 78
public awareness, 46, 48, 62
public officials, 20, 55
public safety, 57
public service, 45
public-private partnerships, 5, 43, 56

## Q

quality of life, 76
quality of service, 5

## R

radio, 12, 45
ramp, 62, 70, 78
rape, 78
reception, 46, 52, 53, 54, 61, 71
recognition, 70
recommendations, 18, 86
recreational, 43
recruiting, 7
reform(s), 8, 41, 43, 47, 57, 58, 63, 67, 71
refugee admission, 65
refugee status, 46, 79
refugees, 38, 60, 62, 78
regional policy, 61
Registry, 53
regulatory systems, 5
rehabilitation, 12, 54
relatives, 76
reliability, 20
remittances, 56
repatriate, 36
requirements, 74
resilience, 81
resolution, 61
resources, 11, 14, 35, 36, 37, 46, 47, 52, 54, 55, 56, 57, 70, 73, 74, 83, 86
response, 6, 7, 8, 9, 11, 15, 16, 17, 18, 20, 38, 43, 45, 51, 60, 62, 64, 69, 71, 75
response capacity, 51
revenue, 49
rights, 40, 60
risk(s), 33, 38, 43, 46, 49, 52, 70, 71, 72, 74, 78, 82, 83, 84, 85
risk factors, 71
root, 38, 51, 55, 61, 70, 71, 72
routes, 58
rule of law, 74, 77
rural areas, 10, 70, 73, 85

rural development, 43
rural schools, 73

## S

safe haven(s), 86
safety, 37, 56, 57, 60, 66, 82
San Salvador, 54
savings, 85
school, 7, 14, 16, 53, 57, 72, 73, 74
schooling, 5
scope, 63, 76, 81
secondary education, 9
Secretary of Commerce, 73
Secretary of Homeland Security, 45
security, 16, 35, 36, 41, 42, 43, 46, 48, 49, 55, 56, 59, 62, 63, 69, 70, 71, 74, 76, 77, 79, 87
security forces, 55
seedlings, 12
seizure, 46
Senate, 34, 47, 68
Senate Committee on the Judiciary, 34
service provider, 56
services, 8, 10, 12, 46, 52, 53, 54, 72, 85, 86
sex, 24, 29, 32
sexual abuse, 7
shape, 11, 17, 36, 87
shelter, 53, 54, 60
small businesses, 84, 85
smuggling, 2, 3, 6, 7, 10, 12, 13, 14, 36, 46, 58, 62, 78
Smuggling, 12, 14, 58, 68
social development, 16, 47
social exclusion, 76
social network, 58
social responsibility, 74
social support, 84
social support network, 84
social welfare, 53
South America, 70
Soviet Union, 40, 41
spending, 47
stability, 83
stakeholders, 11, 76
state(s), 36, 48, 57, 58, 66, 82, 83
stock, 44
structure, 20
support services, 62
surveillance, 60
sustainability, 77, 84

## T

tactics, 7
talent, 86
target, 10, 36, 46, 72, 84
tax rates, 56
tax system, 57
taxes, 56
taxpayers, 70
teacher training, 16
teams, 78
technical assistance, 43, 56
technical comments, 19
technology, 47, 74
territorial, 55
territorial control, 55
territory, 37, 57, 58
The Homeland Security Act, 26
threats, 70, 82
trade, 40, 41, 42, 44, 48
trade agreement, 41
trafficking, 33, 47, 57, 58
trafficking in persons, 33, 58
trainees, 84
training, 43, 48, 52, 59, 72, 74, 83, 85, 87
transparency, 5, 43, 57, 74
transportation, 5, 43, 53, 58
transportation infrastructure, 43

## U

U.S. Agency for International Development, 1, 2, 4, 13, 15, 19, 41, 64, 69
U.S. assistance, 2, 4, 46, 52, 64
U.S. Department of Commerce, 65
U.S. immigration law, 7, 58, 70

U.S. policy, 36, 38, 39, 40, 41, 45, 57, 62, 63, 69
U.S.-Mexican border, vii, 1, 3
UAC, vii, 1, 2, 3, 4, 6, 7, 8, 9, 11, 12, 13, 14, 15, 17, 18, 19, 20, 21, 33, 34, 35, 63
UN, 68
unaccompanied alien children, vii, 1, 2, 3, 23, 24, 25, 26, 27, 28, 29, 30, 31, 32, 33, 35, 63
UNHCR, 52, 53, 59, 60, 61, 62, 64, 66, 68, 78
United, v, vii, 1, 2, 4, 5, 6, 7, 8, 10, 15, 16, 19, 20, 23, 24, 27, 35, 36, 37, 38, 40, 41, 42, 43, 44, 45, 46, 47, 51, 53, 54, 56, 58, 60, 62, 63, 64, 65, 67, 69, 75, 76, 78, 82, 83
United Nations, 4, 10, 64, 78
United Nations High Commissioner for Refugees, 64, 78
United States, v, vii, 1, 2, 4, 5, 6, 7, 8, 10, 15, 16, 19, 20, 23, 24, 27, 35, 36, 37, 38, 40, 41, 42, 43, 44, 45, 46, 47, 51, 53, 54, 56, 58, 60, 62, 63, 64, 65, 67, 69, 75, 76, 78, 82, 83
universities, 10
urban, 6, 9, 70, 73, 83, 84, 86
urban areas, 6, 9, 70
USAID, v, 1, 2, 3, 4, 5, 6, 7, 8, 9, 10, 11, 12, 13, 14, 15, 16, 17, 18, 19, 41, 42, 46, 49, 50, 52, 53, 54, 64, 65, 66, 67, 69, 71, 72, 73, 74

## V

valve, 56
variables, 25, 33
venue, 85
Vice President, 15, 45, 46, 68, 71, 76, 78
victims, 58
violence, 2, 3, 5, 6, 8, 9, 11, 12, 13, 14, 16, 36, 38, 41, 43, 48, 55, 56, 57, 60, 61, 66, 70, 71, 72, 73, 75, 76, 86
violent crime, 16, 55
vision, 77, 79, 87
vocational training, 9, 48, 57, 73, 77, 85
vote, 85

## W

Washington, 17, 20, 21, 67, 68
water, 82
watershed, 83
weakness, 58
White House, 45, 65, 67, 68, 78
workers, 56, 73, 74
workforce, 72, 73
working groups, 3, 17
World Bank, 5
worldwide, 4

## Y

young people, 70, 73, 76, 82, 83, 84, 86
youth populations, 62